THE SHOW MUST GO ON

Rick Sky is the pop music editor of Britain's *Daily Mirror*, and has interviewed almost all the world's top rock stars. He has contributed to dozens of publications all round the world, including *Spin*, *The Chicago Tribune* and *Max*.

THE SHOW MUST GO ON

The Life of
Freddie Mercury

RICK SKY

Fontana
An Imprint of HarperCollinsPublishers

Fontana
An Imprint of HarperCollins*Publishers*
77–85 Fulham Palace Road,
Hammersmith, London W6 8JB

A Fontana Original 1992
9 8 7

Copyright © Rick Sky 1992

The Author asserts the moral right to
be identified as the author of this work

A catalogue record for this book is
available from the British Library

ISBN 0 00637843 9

Set in Linotron Meridien

Printed in Great Britain by
HarperCollinsManufacturing Glasgow

*Dedicated to the memory of
Freddie Mercury, who never stopped enjoying life,
and to Queen fans everywhere*

CONTENTS

CONTENTS

Chapter 1

END OF A LEGEND

The Last Moments of Freddie Mercury

*'If I am dead tomorrow I don't give a damn.
I really have done it all'*

He lay beneath white satin sheets in his king-sized canopied bed, which he had once boasted could comfortably sleep six, all alone but finally looking at peace with the world. The Persian cats he had cradled a few hours before had slunk sadly away. Gone too was the last of the close friends who had visited him faithfully over the previous weeks. The doctors who had attended him had left an hour earlier, and his first girlfriend, Mary Austin, the mother of his twenty-month-old godson Ricky, had kissed him on the cheek with tears in her eyes before rushing out of his magnificent eight-bedroomed mansion into the London night.

Outside the high walls guarding the £4 million Kensington home that had become Freddie Mercury's sanctuary from the world, a legion of fans, newspapermen and TV cameras waited for the end. As he left, one of Mercury doctors, Gordon Atkinson, told insistent reporters that the singer was slipping away. Twenty-four hours earlier, rock's most flamboyant star had issued a statement through his publicity people revealing that he had AIDS. It was a secret he had kept from the world for the previous five years.

Inside, the singer's gaunt grey face, bearing no resemblance now to the proud one that had stared down from millions of posters, lay perfectly still on the pillow. His breathing had slowed and his brown eyes saw only a mist flooding the huge bedroom which occupied much of the third floor of his exquisite home. Next to him sat just one of his most faithful friends, among them sixties pop heart-throb Dave Clark, who was gently holding his hand. It was now as withered as the rest of his wasted and tormented body, a body once so muscular that Freddie would proudly strip off on stage to a pair of shorts as he strutted and preened before his adoring audience.

Mercury was oblivious to it all. For the last two days he could not eat, could barely speak or see. He lay there, little more than a corpse, oblivious to the beautiful antiques, Japanese paintings and French Impressionist masters he had spent hundreds of thousands of pounds on over the years, building a collection that was the envy of art lovers. Oblivious to the cards and letters that his pop peers had sent him saying how he had enriched their lives and how their thoughts and prayers were with him now. Oblivious, even, to the statement that had been put out by his publicist Roxy Meade just twenty-four hours before, when the decision was taken to break the wall of silence that had surrounded him. That statement said simply: 'I wish to confirm I have been tested HIV positive and have

AIDS. I felt it correct to keep this information private to date in order to protect the privacy of those around me. However, the time has now come for my friends and fans around the world to know the truth. I hope everyone will join with me, my doctors and all those worldwide in the fight against this terrible disease.'

Yet when the end finally came, though inevitable, it was still unexpected: Mercury's friends had believed he would hang on for some days yet. It came so quickly that even his parents, Jer and Bomi Bulsara, rushing from their small semi-detached home in Feltham, did not manage to reach their son's bedside in time.

At seven P.M. on that bitter evening of Sunday 24 November, Freddie Mercury's life and reign were over and the rock world became a much smaller and colder place. His death was finally announced at midnight in a short statement which read: 'Freddie Mercury died peacefully this evening at his home. His death was the result of broncho-pneumonia, brought on by AIDS.' A few days later Dave Clark reassured the world that the singer had died happily: 'He didn't say anything. He just went to sleep and passed on. It was very peaceful. He was a rare person, as unique as a painting. I know he has gone to a much better place.'

During the weeks before his death, as Mercury battled against bouts of blindness and severe pneumonia, close friends came to pay their last respects. Among them were Elton John, disc jockey Kenny Everett and the remaining members of Queen.

His ex-girlfriend Mary Austin, for whom he had bought a luxury apartment just minutes away from his own home, came every day. 'He knew the end was coming,' she said through a veil of tears, 'but he kept his sense of humour right to the end. During the last few days he was in great pain and suffered a lot. He couldn't eat and was under heavy sedation. Despite the agony he was going through he told me he had no regrets.

'When I left his bedside, I kissed him on the cheek, held his hand and told him I loved him very much. But the suffering I saw with Freddie I never want to witness again.'

After Mercury died, aged just forty-five, flowers and messages flooded in from almost every major rock star in the world. One of the most moving tributes was from the three remaining members of his band, Brian May, Roger Taylor and John Deacon, who told the world: 'We have lost the greatest and most beloved member of our family. We feel overwhelming grief that he has gone. We all have a great pride in the courageous way that he lived and died. It has been a privilege for us to share such magical times.'

Mercury, known for his generosity, was magnanimous right to the end. A few days after his death, it was announced that he had donated the rights to one of Queen's biggest-selling songs ever, 'Bohemian Rhapsody', to the AIDS charity the Terrence Higgins Trust. The song was going to be rush-released in time for Christmas and pop pundits were predicting that it was certain to be one of the biggest-selling singles of all time.

There were even more tributes and flowers at Mercury's funeral, which took place at the West London crematorium in London's busy Harrow Road four days after his death.

Just like Mercury himself, the occasion, which the singer had spent weeks planning in meticulous detail, was a bewildering mixture of flamboyance and secrecy, witnessing the collision of two very different worlds – the modern world of rock music and the ancient world of the Zoroastrian religion, in which Mercury had been brought up.

Zoroastrianism is one of the world's oldest and most exclusive religions. Founded by the prophet Zoroaster (or Zarathustra) in 1500 B.C. it has only 120,000 members worldwide and just six thousand in Britain. Its followers see life as a battle between two spirits, Spenta Mainyu, the 'Bounteous Spirit', and Angra Mainya, the 'Destructive Spirit'. Whichever one a Zoroastrian lives his life by determines where he or she goes to after death. That final resting place is the Zoroastrian equivalent to the Christian Heaven or Hell.

As Mercury's oak coffin was carried into the chapel, covered in a satin sheet and topped with a single red rose, Zoroastrian priests, dressed in white muslin robes and caps, chanted traditional prayers to their god Ahura Mazda, also known as the Wise Lord, for the salvation of the singer's soul. Throughout the twenty-five minute service, conducted totally in the ancient Avestan language, the priests used no word of English other than commands to the forty mourners to stand and sit.

Mercury had insisted on his funeral being a private, low-key affair and the magical ancient ceremony was attended only by extremely close friends and family, as he had wished. The singer's parents, Bomi and Jer Bulsara, wept throughout as did Mary Austin and Elton John. Among the other tearful mourners were sixties drummer turned impresario Dave Clark, the three remaining members of Queen and Brian May's girlfriend, former EastEnders' soap star Anita Dobson.

Just after nine on that cold wintry morning, a gleaming black Rolls Royce carrying the coffin in which Mercury's body lay drove slowly into the grounds of the West London crematorium in Kensal Rise. It was followed by five Daimler hearses transporting all the flowers and cards that had arrived at Mercury's home from the day of his death. Behind them came a fleet of seven Mercedes limousines carrying the mourners who had come to pay their last respects to one of rock's greatest ever showmen.

Music, which had turned Freddie Mercury from a shy art student into one of the rock world's most charismatic stars, was inevitably an important part of the service. As the coffin was carried in, the strains of soul star Aretha Franklin, one of Mercury's favourite singers, singing the gospel hymn 'Precious Lord, Take My Hand' rose from the stereo system. It was followed by another of her songs, 'You've Got A Friend', one of the most touching and heartfelt songs ever recorded. And as the mourners filed out, the funeral music burst forth once again – this time an aria from a Verdi opera, another of Mercury's passions. It held a very special meaning for the singer because it was sung by a very special friend of his, the Spanish diva Montserrat Caballé, with whom he had duetted on the pair's hit single 'Barcelona'.

As the tearful procession walked past the mass array of flowers, many stopped to read the inscriptions on the wreaths. Stars such as David Bowie, U2 and Gary Glitter had sent floral tributes. Glitter's was a massive star made out of white carnations, a symbol of what Mercury meant to him. The card read: 'Freddie, sadly missed and never forgotten.' Mary Austin had sent a pillow of white and yellow roses with the motto

'For my dearest with my deepest love, from your old faithful', while Dave Clark's inscription read: 'Life is eternal, my friend. Your contribution to the world will be everlasting.' Elton John, whose wreath was in the shape of a heart made out of salmon pink roses, wrote simply: 'Thank you for being my friend. I will love you always.' Another admirer of Mercury's, Boy George, sent the message 'Dear Freddie, I love you.' But the most touching of all was the message from his parents, who were still close to their only son despite the rumours that his life style had upset them and though he had lived the kind of life they could never have imagined or understood. It read simply: 'To our very beloved son Freddie. We love you always. Mum and Dad.'

Chapter 2

EARLY DAYS

From Zanzibar to London

'The bigger, the better – in everything'

For the first fourteen years of his life Farokh Bulsara had some of the world's most exotic places for a playground. It was a fitting dress rehearsal for the man who, in his reincarnation as Freddie Mercury, was to become one of the rock world's most flamboyant showmen.

Mercury's earliest years were spent on two remote, idyllic islands, Zanzibar and Pemba, which lie in the Indian Ocean, off the East Coast of Africa. Both islands were tight-knit, friendly communities and Mercury played out of doors with the other children in perfect safety, enjoying the warm sea, miles of golden beaches and long hours of sunlight. Pemba was so remote that when Mercury's family lived there it had no electricity. To get news of the outside world his father Bomi had to walk to a friend's home and try to tune into the World Service on his wireless.

Until he was seven, when his sister Kashmira was born, Freddie (the English translation of Farokh) was an only child and the apple of his parents' eye. They had plenty of time to indulge him because life on those faraway islands was slow and relaxed. Mr Bulsara was a clerk in the judiciary and finished work every day at one-thirty, when he and his wife, Jer, would take their young son down to the beach to let him paddle in the water and teach him to swim. From time to time they also took him to the gardens attached to the Zanzibar museum, a favourite spot for young parents to take their children.

Back home they read him fairy stories, stories of genies, princes and pirates, which would have seemed all the more real to Freddie in that exotic landscape. One book that particularly thrilled him was *The Arabian Nights*, whose characters were Persian just like him. There was never any shortage of people to play with or read stories to Freddie, since the family were rich enough, as he later frequently boasted, to have servants who indulged the young child's every whim.

When he was five years old Freddie was taken to another exotic place, the teeming Indian city of Bombay with its bustling marketplaces and colourful bazaars. His family had originally gone to Zanzibar from Bombay, which, like Pemba and Zanzibar, was once part of Britain's huge and mighty colonial empire, and Freddie's father now decided that his son should live in Bombay because it had some of the best schools in that part of the world.

Mercury's parents were both Parsees and devout followers of the Zoroastrian religion and it was in Bombay that the largest Parsee community in the world was to be found. In the tenth century, after the Islamic invasion of Persia, the Parsees fled to India, where they were free to practise their religion. India had a reputation as one of the most tolerant countries in the world when it came to religion and in Bombay, with its polyglot population, many of the world's religious groups – Hindus, Muslims, Christians, Sikhs, Jains and Zoroastrians – lived side by side.

The Parsees were one of the most economically successful communities in Bombay. In their early days they had adopted the language and dress of India's largest religious group, the Hindus, but they later exchanged them for the customs and way of life of India's former colonial masters, the British. So the young Freddie was to receive a typical British public school education, even if it was achieved thousands of miles away from Eton and Harrow.

India, at the time the young Mercury arrived, had a population of four hundred million and Bombay was its largest city – and the world's seventh biggest. A harbour port lying on its western seaboard overlooking the Arabian Sea, it was the country's financial and commercial centre. Bombay was a fantastic place for Freddie to grow up in. He loved playing in its winding, narrow streets and visiting the beautiful Hanging Gardens in the affluent Malabar Hill area close by the Parsee hospital. He loved going to the bazaar to watch the snake charmers weave their magical, hypnotic tunes, or to gape wide-eyed at the fakirs, Indian holy men, lying on their beds of nails. In those crammed markets he would watch the traders sell the city's most exotic wares as he feasted on mangoes, coconuts and lychees. In the afternoon he would go to the harbour and look out on to a sea of ships laden with tea, cotton and rice ready to set off on voyages to distant parts.

Mercury enjoyed his boarding school too. He excelled

in sport, particularly cricket, boxing and table tennis. The fast, furious pace of table tennis – involving a mixture of dexterity and speed – was something he was especially skilled in and he became one of the school champions at the sport. It was at school in Bombay that Mercury also began the piano lessons which were to be crucial to those florid, bombastic compositions for which Queen became known. The city was a bizarre musical melting pot, where the eleven-year-old was simultaneously exposed to the classics and operas that his cultured parents loved, the meandering rhythms and romance of Indian music and a pinch of that relatively new phenomenon, rock and roll, which was slowly beginning to invade the world.

Religion, too, played an important role in Mercury's life and he went with other Zoroastrian youngsters to the fire temples where the Parsees worship. The sacred fires are a crucial part of their religion and prayers are said in front of them as an affirmation of a believer's faith. They are kept permanently burning – in some parts of Iran there are fires that are two thousand years old – and are tended five times a day by the priests of the temple.

At the age of eight Freddie became a full member of the Zoroastrian religion in the majestic Navjote ceremony, during which the young initiate was given a purifying bath while the head priest chanted prayers. (The bath symbolises physical cleanliness, which devotees regard as essential for the cleansing of the mind and soul.) Then, in front of one of the eternal fires, he repeated the prayers of the priests, accepting the Zoroastrian religion as revealed by Ahura Mazda to Zoroaster, and was given his *sudreh*, a shirt made out of white muslin, symbol of innocence and purity.

Around his waist the priest then tied the *kusti*, a cord made out of the finest and purest white lamb's wool and symbolising the girding of the loins to serve humanity. The *kusti* was wrapped around him three times to remind the young boy of the three aspects of Ahura Mazda as creator, preserver and reconstructor and the initiate was expected to wear it for the rest of his life. Finally Mercury was showered with rice, rose petals, coconut and pomegranate and dressed in his new clothes. Rusi Dalal, a friend of Mercury's family says of the Navjote ceremony: 'It is one of the most important events in the religion and everyone from the Parsee community is invited. It is a very festive and enjoyable event.'

Later Freddie was to talk affectionately about his years at boarding school. Many pop stars recall their schooldays as a horrific period which they could not wait to finish, but not so Mercury: 'My time at boarding school was very enjoyable. One thing boarding schools teach you is how to fend for yourself and I did that from a very early age. It taught me to be independent and not to have to rely on anybody else.

'We studied everything at school, but the things I liked best were the more artistic subjects like art and literature. The school had a very strong emphasis on sport and I ended up doing every single one of them. I did boxing, cricket and table tennis, which I was really good at.'

In his piano lessons he got as far as passing his grade five examinations. 'I took piano lessons at school and really enjoyed it,' he said. 'That was my mother's doing. She made sure I stuck at it.

'At first I kept up lessons because I knew she wanted me to, but then I really loved playing.'

One of the people to whom Freddie talked about his Indian schooldays was Queen's fan club organizer, Jacky Gunn, who remarked: 'From the way Freddie described it, that school in India sounded wonderful. He seemed to have joined in with a lot of the activities, made some good friends and had a good time there.'

Mercury's world was to turn upside down, however, when, at the age of fourteen, he moved with his family to Britain. Feltham, Middlesex, where they were to settle in a modest semi-detached house, was worlds away from what he had become used to – the carefree, lazy days and long hours of sunshine, the colourful bazaars and street life, the servants. Feltham in 1959 was scarcely an attractive proposition to a worldly thirteen-year-old. Everyday Mercury would join the crowd of drab passengers queuing up for the red double-decker bus that took him to his school in Isleworth, where the other kids made fun of his strange, swarthy looks and his clipped colonial accent. Mercury never referred to those grammar school days in the early interviews he gave, but he clearly disliked their grey uniformity and conservatism. His education suffered and when he left his Isleworth school the only subject he had really excelled in was art.

When he was nineteen Britain was feeling the first rumbles of what were to be known as the 'swinging sixties'. Teenagers throughout the country, even in Feltham, were beginning to cast off their parents' old values, morals and life styles, eager for a different life fuelled by their own fashion, music and money. This was the era of the Mod, a British teen cult who worshipped clothes (adopting in particular, smart Italian fashion), black American rhythm and blues and soul music and thought nothing of spending an entire week's pay packet on such essentials to their life style. It was also the era of the Beatles and the Rolling Stones. In 1965 three bands were battling it out with each other for chart domination. The Beatles scored three number one hits with 'I Feel Fine', 'Ticket To Ride' and 'Day Tripper', while the Rolling Stones matched them with three chart-toppers of their own, 'The Last Time', 'Satisfaction' and 'Get Off My Cloud'.

Black soul music was ruling the charts too. Otis Redding had a big hit with 'My Girl'; Wilson Pickett scored with 'In The Midnight Hour', and the Supremes hit the charts four times, their biggest hit that year being 'Stop In The Name Of Love'. And a new London group the Who, formed not far from where Mercury lived, made their first foray into the charts with 'I Can't Explain'. Their sharp clothes and brash rhythm and blues based sounds made them the darling of the Mods, and guitarist Pete Townshend's anthem 'My Generation' summed up what it was like to be a teenager in London during those exciting times.

It was a time when pop music was trying to break out of the narrow confines in which it had been locked and to show that it was more than a throwaway piece of candyfloss for lovesick teenagers. Occupying the vanguard of this new 'intelligent' rock was the former folk troubadour Robert Zimmerman, better known as Bob Dylan, whose album *Bringing It All Back Home* was to influence thousands of lyric writers all around the world and change the course of rock music for ever.

The year 1965 was the beginning of youth protest and drug experimentation. In America thousands of youngsters had burned their draft cards in protest over the Vietnam War while a prankster called Ken Kessey began group experiments with the then still legal hallucinogen lysergic acid in the first of his aptly named Acid Tests.

In Britain many of the movers in the fashion and rock world were the product of the art schools. The majority of the Stones, the most rebellious rock band the world had ever seen, had come out of them, and the Who's Svengali, their guitar-wrecking leader Pete Townshend, had decided to form his band during his days at Ealing Art School, the college nineteen-year-old Freddie had set his sights on. Art schools represented freedom, creativity and the chance for students to 'do their own thing'. Mercury's parents did not particularly like the idea of their only son going to one, but strong-willed Freddie got his own way. He hoped it would help him retrieve some of that magic, colour and excitement he had left behind in Zanzibar and India.

The other students around velvet-trousered Frederick Bulsara were deep in thought designing a new detergent package. Twenty-year-old Freddie had drawn a few scribbles on his page and then drifted off into a daydream. Trying to get people to buy soap powder was not the life he saw for himself. He dreamed of the day he would be selling something more potent and magical . . . himself as a rock superstar.

Slowly he got up on his platform-stacked shoes and grasped his twelve-inch ruler with both hands, his right one pushing the narrow piece of plastic onto his groin. His left hand weaved up and down playing a series of imaginary notes and his swarthy lean face contorted into an expression of rapture.

Opening his buck-toothed mouth he sang 'Purple Haze all in my brain . . .' Jimi Hendrix's chart-topping single. Hendrix had become rock's most flamboyant star, an icon of Britain's underground culture, and Mercury was besotted by the wild-haired, wild-living Seattle guitarist who had made his home in the still-swinging English capital.

Obsessed by everything about Hendrix – from the rainbow-coloured silk shirts and chiffon scarves he wore to the hairstyle that looked as if it was the result of a dozen electric shocks – to Mercury the half Cherokee Indian star summed up everything that was exciting, dangerous and passionate about being young.

At art school he would spend a lot of his time painting pictures of the outrageous guitarist, his favourite picture of Hendrix showed him as a fashionable fop dressed in eighteenth-century high fashion. Later on in interviews Mercury would cite the unlikely combination of Hendrix and Liza Minelli as his two main influences.

Six years on he would be using a cut-off microphone stand in place of a plastic ruler, playing it as an imaginary guitar and leaving thousands of fans screaming for more. But today his pop performance did not bring the house down. 'Sit down Bulsara, you're rubbish. You couldn't sing your way out of a paper bag,' mocked one student. He was not alone in his opinion. Fellow student Jerry Hibbert, now a company director, remembers: 'Freddie was a quiet chap at art school. It was quite a shock when he turned out to be such a big star. There were other students at college who were far more flamboyant and louder than him. And Graham Collis, now a film director, recalls Mercury as being a bit of a 'drip'. 'He was quite wet and used to giggle like schoolgirl. We didn't think he was particularly talented. When he used to stand up and mimic Jimi Hendrix we used to shout him down saying: "Sit down Freddie, you'll never be a success."'

Graham Rose, in the same graphics class as Freddie recalls that the singer's future sartorial style – the leotards, the ermine capes and the catsuits – wasn't in evidence at all. 'Freddie wasn't an outrageous flamboyant personality at all. He was as skinny as a pencil and he used to wear tight jeans or crushed velvet trousers which made him even skinnier. But what he wore was no different from what we were all wearing around that time. On the whole he was a quiet guy, though he was prone to fits of giggles. When that happened he would put his hand right over his mouth to cover up those huge teeth of his. I remember him as a terrific bloke who was very sweet and considerate. There wasn't a nasty streak in him. A lot of us were very pleased when he went on to be such a great success.'

And of Mercury had plenty of wild living and wild loving days during Queen's reign in the pop world, he did not appear to have any at college. His friends at Ealing can remember very few girlfriends and no boyfriends. Former classmate Rosemary Collis did a fashion course which Freddie was on for a year: 'I can't remember him being particularly popular with girls'. And he too left little impression on her. 'Freddie only stood out because he was one of only two boys in our class. He was terribly quiet and unassuming. He certainly never wore anything outrageous,' she says.

Mercury was quite distant from the rest of his boisterous class, according to a former teacher at Ealing College of Art. At times lessons would turn into pandemonium, but the embryonic singer was never one of the troublemakers, says printmaking tutor Peter Daglish: 'Freddie always appeared a bit removed from the others. He seemed to keep himself to himself. I think he felt a bit different, possibly because of his foreign looks. But he certainly did not ostracise himself from the others.'

At times the students were a bunch of rowdies, says Daglish, but Mercury did not run with the pack: 'On one occasion I had to read out the riot act to them. It was in the afternoon and I don't know if they had been drinking in a pub or what they had been up to, but they were very loud. The more boisterous members of the group included Tim Staffell and Graham Rose.

'Lots of students were into music. Graham Rose used to sing loudly and enthusiastically and Tim Staffell was another clown. They had that kind of schoolboy mentality to a degree. Sometimes the group was very loud and would take the piss out of the tutor, but it was quite harmless.'

'The only time I do remember Freddie larking about,' adds Daglish, 'he was standing at the back of the class miming Jimi Hendrix and using a T-square as a microphone. I was very surprised when Freddie became such a star.'

According to Daglish, the course had a good reputation and it was hard to get on it. Most students went on to be successful in a wide range of areas, including film making, advertising, design, illustration, painting, fine art and photography. 'It was a very forward-thinking course. All the tutors on the foundation course practised what they taught. There were similar courses around, but they did not have the same sort of dynamism. It was a great experience to teach there and Freddie's year were a very talented lot.

'The assignments they were given were very creative. We gave students an idea and they had to respond to the brief by bringing as much invention as they could to it.'

Among the assignments Mercury's class were given was one called 'The Queen's Garden Party'. The students had to create imaginary guests for the party and then do portraits of them. It was the first Queen party that Mercury had been involved in and – though he couldn't know it at the time – a portent of things to come.

Chapter 3

SMILE

The Beginning of Queen
and a Unique Musical Style

*'If I didn't do this, I wouldn't have
anything to do. I can't cook.
I'm not very good at being a housewife'*

The band almost fell by the wayside, like so many others. The group's first tentative steps into the world of rock were taken way back in 1968, but it took another six years of struggling for recognition and battling against the bad reviews before success was in sight. Their career began in the corridors of London's Imperial College, where Brian May was a physics student trying to put together a band. A former dentistry student, Roger Taylor, and an art student, Tim Staffell, were quick to join and they called themselves Smile. An American label signed them up for a one-off contract and the band looked forward to its big break.

The first single, which was also to be Smile's last, was a complete flop, partly because it was only released in the United States with no group or record company support. In 1970 Staffell left the group to try his luck with another band called Humpy Bong, who he believed had what it took to become a success. He managed to persuade a former art student colleague of his, Freddie Mercury, to join Smile. Mercury had previously sung for two other relatively unknown bands, Wreckage and Sour Milk Sea. In that year the three plus what was to become a series of bass players embarked on tours of England's colleges and clubs.

After the group had worked their way unsuccessfully through six bassists they signed up John Deacon, who became the fourth member of the band in 1971. The group acquired its new name, Queen, thought up by Mercury several years before. He explained: 'It's just a name but it's very regal, obviously, and it sounds splendid. It's a strong name, very universal and immediate.'

. Queen's big break came in 1972, as an indirect result of the many studio demos they made at De Lane Lea recording studios, where they were asked to test out equipment in return for unlimited studio time. These tapes were rejected by a number of big record companies and it was not until they began playing at London's various pubs and clubs that the band were spotted by executives from Trident Audio Productions. They signed a publishing, production and management deal which resulted in their being signed up with the giant EMI company. Now at last Queen were on the road to stardom – even if they could have no inkling of it at this stage, given the reception of the debut single 'Keep Yourself Alive'. Amid accusations of hype, Radio One refused to put it on their play list and it failed to get into the charts. The debut album flopped as well, with many critics making vicious comments ('a bucket of urine' – Nick Kent in the *NME*), but became a hit a year later after the success of their second LP, *Queen II*.

Arduous rounds of tours and appearances eventually began to pay off and by 1974 the band's growing following and hit single 'Seven Seas of Rhye' were the proof that Queen had made it. They were to keep on making it and grow musically fatter, more confident and more adventurous with every year. They managed to hold their heads as high as Mercury did during his performances, despite the onslaught of musical fads which saw the death of many bands. They outlived disco, punk rock and the latest teen-age bands.

They also saw the need for sabbatical breaks from each other in order to engage in a variety of other projects. Mercury made a number of solo records, among them 'Love Kills' in 1984, (though eleven years earlier he had made 'I Can Hear the Music' under the pseudonym Larry Lurex) which hit the top ten. His biggest solo single success was with 'The Great Pretender', which climbed to number four in March 1987. His debut solo album, *Mr Bad Guy*, recorded in Munich, did well too, reaching number ten in May 1985. The singer's solo work also included a couple of songs for the West End musical *Time*, as well as his album *Barcelona* with Spanish opera star Montserrat Caballé.

Roger Taylor was the first member of the band to branch out on a solo career under his own name, releasing a single, 'I Wanna Testify', in August 1977, and was even more prolific away from the band than Mercury was. He released the albums *Fun In Space* in 1981 and *Strange Frontier* in 1984 and got back to his rock and roll roots with a band he formed called the

Cross, which went out on the road as well as releasing two albums, *Shove It* and *Mad, Bad And Dangerous To Know*.

Brian May turned session musician and producer, working with such diverse talents as Bad News (the comedy heavy metal group featuring the stars of the Young Ones) and Anita Dobson (former EastEnders' barmaid), while also recording some tracks as part of Star Fleet Project, who brought out a mini LP in October 1983. And bassist John Deacon, who was responsible for some of the band's biggest hits, including 'Another One Bites The Dust', formed the Immortals in order to write music for the motion picture *Biggles*. It demonstrated to the world that he, like the other members of the band, had a musical identity and talent of his own which stopped him from ever growing stale within the group.

Queen were prolific in output too at a time when far less successful bands often took four years to record an album. They released an LP a year on average from 1973 to 1991 – a feat few modern or established bands achieve.

Although he was the best-known member of Queen, Freddie Mercury was not Queen. The three other members, Brian May, Roger Taylor and John Deacon, were not his backing group; each was an essential ingredient of the band as a whole, and the band could only function as a result of their joint contributions. Each of them was a talented musician in his own right, especially May, whose innovative guitar work was as much a trademark of Queen's songs as Mercury's distinctive vocal style. Each wrote songs, each was fully involved in the band's gruelling recording sessions, and each had a vision of what he wanted the band to become.

Even Mercury's love of partying was not uniquely his. Drummer Roger Taylor, whose blond good looks once made him the band's pin-up, gave Mercury a very good run when it came to wild living. And though Mercury's sharp intelligence made him a great spokesman, it did not set him apart from the rest of the group either. All of them had degrees and their academic prowess had got them dubbed the boffins of rock. In their way, they were all spokesmen for the band and its music, but if Mercury was the one who naturally grabbed the headlines, the rest of the group, unlike a lot of bands, were not jealous of it, but happy to let him bask in the limelight.

The key to the band's success – a success that kept them at the top for almost twenty years and resulted in sales of a hundred million records – was their musical versatility. Though they had an identifiable sound, their songs were never stuck in a rut but were as varied as Mercury's ever-changing wardrobe. Much has been written about their fusion of rock music and opera, as in their mouldbreaking 'Bohemian Rhapsody', with its heady mix of operatic choruses and screeching guitar. But their songs were much more than Carmen meeting Led Zeppelin and living to tell the tale.

Queen could make hard rock songs to match any heavy metal band. 'Tie Your Mother Down' was one. They could make stadium rock full of chants and crescendos like 'We Are The Champions'. They could make great disco records like 'Another One Bites The Dust' and 'Under Pressure'. They created futuristic electronic sounds, as in the mesmerising 'Radio GaGa', and gentle rock ballads, as in 'It's A Kind Of Magic' and the posthumous 'These are the Days Of Our Lives', one of the most moving songs the band ever recorded. They produced high camp in 'Fat Bottomed Girls' and majestic overblown manifestos like 'I Want To Break Free'. They wrote songs with powerful messages like 'One Vision' and songs with no message at all. They could even pastiche Elvis and make the sound their own, as in 'Crazy Little Thing Called Love', a song whose very simplicity makes it hard to believe it was written by the same man who penned the complex and meandering 'Bohemian Rhapsody'.

Year in, year out, Queen were able to create new and exciting songs which captivated an ever-increasing audience that never showed any real signs of tiring. In a career which spanned nineteen albums their range of musical styles seemed almost endless, and they were constantly exploring new directions and new horizons – always entertainingly, if not always successfully. To remain in the vanguard of rock for almost twenty years meant that Queen had to keep reinventing themselves and their music. Along the way they had constantly to make sure they never fell into two of pop's biggest pitfalls – becoming dated and appealing purely to a hard core of fans. That they did all that and wove a complex web of musical styles while still retaining an identifiable sound is an achievement to which few other bands can lay claim – and all the more praiseworthy for occurring in an era where musical styles and fashions change overnight.

But Mercury laid down the Queen manifesto early on in the band's career: 'I like to deliberately do things that aren't considered Queen. I always believe in doing something different. Otherwise what's the point? You might as well give out copies of your old records. I always want to work on things that haven't been done before. It makes it so interesting and you get a real freshness out of it.'

The fans loved the band's constant changes. At its peak the British arm of the Queen fan club boasted a staggering forty-seven thousand members. Queen's enigma was that though they could produce a record that you hated, their next release could totally charm you. They managed to survive despite mistakes, embarrassments, slatings and constant pigeonholing. 'I hate being labelled,' Mercury once said. 'Labels just bounce off me. Music should be one open door.'

Every Queen album was a kind of magic to the band's ever-growing army of fans all around the world. And each conjured up some rare musical feasts. During the two decades the band were together they stretched the boundaries of rock music to their fullest, blending opera, funk and dance and producing an aural wonderland which will still remain fresh and zestful fifty years on. Though Mercury was the band's most prolific songwriter (his *pièce de résistance* being 'Bohemian Rhapsody'), all the members of the band were talented composers and all contributed to Queen's seemingly endless supply of hits. From Brian May came such hits as 'We Will Rock You'. Roger Taylor penned 'Radio GaGa', while John Deacon was responsible for 'I Want To Break Free'. Between them they made sure that each album had plenty of gems on it.

Their first LP, *Queen*, did not take the charts by storm and even its most impressive track, their first single, 'Keep Yourself Alive', failed to make the top forty. But the album planted enough seeds to ensure that this was a band who were going to be a major force in rock music. Apart from Mercury's voice the album highlighted some incredibly adventurous guitar work and it was that guitar based sound which launched Queen into the hard rock scene as a kind of Glam Rock version of Led Zeppelin. It was a hard rock sound that was to take some time for the group to shake off, though they eventually managed to do so by mellowing the harmonies and cutting down the metal-dominated feel. But though the group hated being labelled and wanted more than anything else to be original, that musical niche did create for them an audience whose backing they needed to ensure their records kept selling.

When *Queen II* appeared in March 1974, 'Seven Seas Of Rhye' began forging its way up the charts and the group experienced their first taste of mass exposure. The single fitted perfectly into the charts of the time, which saw the likes of T Rex and Slade take their guitar-based rock to the top. Yet though 'Seven Seas Of Rhye' became Queen's first hit, the accompanying album proved to be a slight but still insignificant improvement on its predecessor. The single was undoubtedly the highlight among other pompously ornate tracks such as 'Ogre Battle' and the 'Fairy Fellers Masterstroke'. Although the band's production had improved, the real magic of Queen had yet to break.

As 1974 progressed the band released the album which finally demonstrated their true potential. *Sheer Heart Attack* came just eight months after the *Queen II* album and convinced even the doubting bassist John Deacon that Queen had something special. 'As I was the last one to join up I was able to view things more from the outside,' he said. 'The band always had a potential to happen in a big way but it wasn't till *Sheer Heart Attack* that I was convinced we would.' The album, a massive improvement on previous offerings, contained the classic 'Killer Queen', a track which encompassed all the harmonic qualities of the foursome. It switched from one musical direction to another in the space of seconds, yet flowed seamlessly along. It deservedly followed 'Seven Seas' into the top ten and narrowly missed giving the band their first UK number one, stalling at number two. The strength of that Mercury-penned track, which resembled 'Bohemian Rhapsody' in construction, gave them the confidence to experiment with other music forms. Along with Brian May's 'Now I'm Here', another chart smash (number eleven), the album demonstrated that Queen could script finely crafted tunes that were elaborate yet had enough catchy hooks in them to ensure they could be easily digested.

By the time *A Night At The Opera* appeared in 1975 the music world knew it had rock royalty in its presence. The album's tour de force was 'Bohemian Rhapsody', one of the most innovative and breathtaking songs ever to have come out of rock. When it was released in late October 1975 'Bohemian Rhapsody' stayed at the top of the charts for nine weeks, a record that was not to be beaten until Bryan Adams's 'Everything I Do I Do It For You', which hit the top spot in the summer and autumn that Mercury was battling for his life. The record became the first Queen single to reach number one and it thrust the band into the public eye as rock's new movers and shapers. Until then they were in danger of being dismissed as little more than pretentious glam rockers, an uneasy mutation of Led Zeppelin and Mud. Although they had already notched up three hit singles

('Seven Seas of Rhye', 'Killer Queen' and 'Now I'm Here'), the group were aware that they were not achieving their full potential. This frustration had coincided with a growing disillusionment with their management company at the time, and so they had decided to sign up with Elton John's tenacious and successful manager, John Reid. The deal was signed just a few weeks before 'Bohemian Rhapsody' was released.

The song was from Queen's album *A Night At The Opera* and it was masterminded by Mercury with the help of producer Roy Thomas Baker. When Baker first heard the rudiments of 'Bohemian Rhapsody' he was stunned. Mercury began to play the framework of the piece on his piano, and then with a royal flourish he informed the bemused producer: 'Now, dear, this is where the opera section comes in.' To incorporate two completely different styles of music in the space of a pop single was unusual and something that generally spelt disaster, but not only was Mercury undeterred, he wanted to run with the idea as long as he could. What was at first expected to be a small insertion of opera escalated into an extravaganza of more than a hundred and eighty voices on tape. It took him three weeks to record, with Mercury making continual changes and additions. According to Baker, 'Freddie would keep adding and changing the operatic section. He knew how he wanted it to sound and wouldn't give up till it was perfect.' Yet despite all the bombast and operetta the rock feel remained and somehow the two forms managed to harmonize.

If Mercury had overcome the difficulty of fusing two very disparate forms of music, the result posed another problem. The final version of 'Bohemian

Rhapsody' that Mercury and the band had produced lasted just under six minutes – more than twice the length of an average single. This and the record's unusual hybridisation of styles caused EMI chiefs apoplexy. Forget that listeners would get bored, they reasoned, a single this length would never get the necessary air time to ensure a hit. But Mercury and Queen, united in their belief in their magnum opus, refused to shorten the track or make any changes. 'We were adamant that "Bohemian Rhapsody" could be a hit in its entirety. We are willing to compromise in many things, but butchering a song is not one of them,' said Mercury.

Despite all the bravado, however, Mercury did harbour secret doubts. These were apparently voiced to Kenny Everett, then a DJ at Radio One. Everett, a good friend of Mercury's, asked to see an unofficial copy of the track, which was leaked to him. The popular and influential DJ loved it and was certain that the public would as well. He said later: 'I knew straightaway it had number one written all over it and it didn't matter one bit how long it was.'

Everett played the song constantly amid a growing public demand which eventually forced EMI to put the record out. It was the first single that the band had released for almost ten months and on the strength of it they were to become a major force in the rock world.

But if the public were enthusiastic about this new sound, many critics weren't. They called it over-produced, pretentious, pure nonsense. Nevertheless, the record hit the top spot a month later. It knocked off comedian Billy Connolly's spoof of Tammy Wynette's country hit 'D.I.V.O.R.C.E' and followed earlier big hits of the year such as David Bowie's 'Space Oddity' and Rod Stewart's 'Sailing'. The record was also the harbinger of the rock video revolution and is generally accepted as being the first true pop video – even if that came about by accident. The band failed to make a spot on 'Top Of The Pops', the most important British TV pop programme when it comes to record sales, and made a film of themselves singing the song instead, commissioning film director Bruce Gowers to make an accompanying promotional video which could be used in its place.

The film cost £5,000 to make and it became the talk of the rock world and pop fans for months to come. These days, of course, it would be unthinkable to spend such a lowly sum on a video – Michael Jackson's for 'Black Or White', the first single from his *Dangerous* album, cost a staggering £4 million to make – but at that time £5,000 was a massive investment on the part of record company EMI. When the video was aired on 'Top Of The Pops' pop fans were left wide-eyed as they saw the band's heads soar around the screen, their faces stretched and multiplied in a jumble of kaleidoscopic effects, all in time with the music.

Record executives could not run the risk of dismissing Queen's promotional film as a one-off advertising gimmick. After all, the song had stayed at number one for nine weeks and there was no doubt that the film had helped keep it there. Queen's *Bohemian Rhapsody* mini-film was the shape of things to come in the pop world. From then on every band had to think seriously about making a video of their latest song if they wanted a hit. *A Night at the Opera* followed up all that *Sheer Heart Attack* had promised the year before. With Roy Thomas Baker at the helm, it contained two further masterpieces. 'You're My Best Friend', a John

Deacon composition, managed to crack the market on both sides of the Atlantic, following in the footsteps of 'Killer Queen', which also made the US top twenty. But for many one of the album's jewels was the ballad 'Love Of My Life', which saw release and success in many countries, although it never made the dent it should have on the UK charts (released as a live track in 1979, it only reached number sixty-three). The song was brought vividly to life when the band performed in Brazil and, such was its power, the crowd sang it word-perfect.

Enthralling the pop world by their dexterity, Queen followed up with another album title taken from a Marx Brothers movie, *A Day At The Races*. Almost exactly a year after *A Night At The Opera*, the album spawned yet another string of great rock tracks, including the barnstorming 'Tie Your Mother Down' and the no-nonsense 'Good Old-Fashioned Loverboy'. 'Somebody To Love', with its over-layered vocals, proved the album's biggest success and secured another number two position for the band in the British charts. (They had to get permission from Groucho Marx to use the movie titles for the albums. Groucho's response to their request read: 'I am very pleased you have named one of your albums after my film and that you are being successful. I would be very happy for you to call your next one after my latest film, The Greatest Hits Of The Rolling Stones')

Album number six, *News Of The World*, released in 1977, resulted in two of the band's best-known and best-loved anthems. The two stadium rockers, 'We Will Rock You' and 'We Are The Champions', were the first two on the album and gave Queen yet another dimension. Both have chorus lines as

powerful as armlocks, and the public happily surren-
dered to them.

The 1978 *Jazz* album did not see the band venturing
into Miles Davis territory, but there was enough
diverse material on it to justify the title. It was a
mixed bag, ranging from the ballad 'Leaving Home
Ain't Easy' to the upbeat 'Bicycle Race' and including
the breathless 'Don't Stop Me Now' and the baroque
camp of 'Fat Bottomed Girls'.

After *Jazz* came *The Game* (1980), which marked
a return to studio albums after a two-year break
and yielded more gems in the form of 'Save Me',
a powerful ballad in which Freddie stretched his
vocal range to the full, and 'Crazy Little Thing Called
Love', an Elvis pastiche which saw Mercury make
his debut as a rhythm guitarist. But the real show
stopper was 'Another One Bites The Dust'. With its
funky beat and breathtaking bass line, it broke new
musical barriers as Queen ventured into a market
normally occupied by black disco artists. The massive
success of the record demonstrated how pigeonholing
the band was unwise. Queen simply refused to be
labelled.

Making sure they kept pace with modern trends,
the band introduced the then current fad of using a
synthesizer for the first time on their records. However,
they didn't overuse the electronic gadgetry, like so
many others, and clung very strongly to their real
instrument base while effectively combining it with
the new technology.

Then came an unusual turn in the band's career,
and one which would give them a whole new audience
– movie goers. In 1980 they heralded the new decade
by undertaking the task of composing the soundtrack

to a major motion picture, which brought to life cartoon strip superhero Flash Gordon. In those days rock and film collaborations were not commonplace – the film world had not yet discovered the power of a specially commissioned pop soundtrack – but Mercury, Taylor, May and Deacon were so impressed when shown rough cuts of the movie they couldn't wait to start work on this new challenge. It was a thoroughgoing success and proved to their fellow artists that you could do a brand-new soundtrack and get a hit record into the bargain. 'Flash', a clever mix of sampling lines from the movie and a thunderbolt chorus, flew up the singles charts, while the album made the number ten spot. It was interesting to see how the band would fare without the overwhelming presence of Mercury's vocals, but May and the rest came through unscathed and with an album held up mainly by their strong instrumentation.

The film's director, Mike Hodges, recalled: 'Queen had this immense sense of fun and recognizable sound, which was what we wanted on *Flash Gordon*. The band liked the film and working on it allowed them to let all their childlike qualities out.'

Queen spent about three months in 1980 working on the fantasy adventure about the comic strip superhero and then three weeks recording the music, also making a video for the single 'Flash'. 'It was great fun working with the band,' says Hodges, 'and there were never any conflicts. In fact everyone was very supportive of each other.'

After the band first saw the film they went away to write the music. And over the period of three months they returned to the film makers sometimes independently and sometimes as a group with their musical pieces. Mercury worked tirelessly, with the same energy and dynamism with which he approached all his projects. According to Hodges, 'He was very meticulous and he thought seriously about things before he started working on them. Although the rest of the band were all involved in the project, Freddie had the strongest visual idea of what was needed. Most of the visual ideas came from him.'

Not only was Mercury a brilliant musician, he was also a natural performer. But coupled with these was also an impatient perfectionist: 'He wasn't called Freddie Mercury for nothing, as he was truly mercurial,' says Hodges. 'As a performer he was operating on all cylinders. He had an extraordinary use of his physique, and his sense of timing was immaculate. He was very confident and seemed to know what would work. He was also very explosive and he got impatient with himself and others when he wanted things to happen immediately. He was also a perfectionist who wanted everything absolutely right.'

But Mercury appeared to be an entirely different person when he wasn't acting as rock's showman: 'When Freddie was not performing he was very modest and quite shy. He was surprisingly small and vulnerable, which made one want to protect him. When I saw him perform on stage I was astonished, as he was extraordinary to watch.'

'I gather Freddie used quite a lot of substances,' Hodges adds. 'But if he did use anything he was incredibly discreet, as I didn't witness anything. From my experience he and the rest of the group were a very professional, sensible band.'

With a worldwide audience ranging from heavy metal fans to youngsters hooked on the Flash Gordon movie, the stage was very much set for the band's next release – *Queen – The Greatest Hits*. It proved a milestone and the biggest-selling 'Best Of' collection of all time. Featuring a slew of ten top ten hits, including the number one 'Bohemian Rhapsody', it brought together the cream of Queen and showcased perfectly the band's breath taking range of vocals and instrumentation. The album was released over a decade ago but the timelessness of its music means that it will never date.

Flushed with the success of their *Greatest Hits* package, the band powered into a brand-new album which was to boast one of rock's most exciting collaborations – Queen and David Bowie. To have two of the most gifted rock acts working together proved irresistible, and their unlikely duet, 'Under Pressure', rocketed to the top slot in the British Singles chart.

The album that featured the mesmeric 'Under Pressure' was *Hot Space*, which was released in 1982 and heralded yet another new direction for Queen as they set out to conquer the dance scene. The band had already had one monster disco hit with the Deacon-penned 'Another One Bites The Dust', but this time around they wanted floor fillers galore. The album contained plenty, including 'Back Chat', 'Body Language' and 'Las Palabras De Amor', but surprisingly the partnership with Bowie was the only top ten hit from the LP and many fans were taken aback by the sudden change in style. The band were undaunted, however, relishing their exploration of fresh sounds.

After *Hot Space* Queen did not release another studio album for two years, during which time all four members pursued solo projects. It was a beneficial break: when they returned to the fold they produced one of their best albums ever. *The Works* of 1984 not only captured a new and younger audience, it also became the band's most successful album up to then. It generated a line of massive chart hits, ranging from the sci-fi of 'Radio GaGa' to the rock stomp of 'Hammer To Fall', which had Brian May writing credits plastered over every note. Other big hits off the LP were 'It's A Hard Life' and 'I Want To Break Free', which featured Mercury at his finest, soaring above the instruments in this song of abandon and emancipation which became an anthem to fans under repressive regimes all over the world, especially in South America and South Africa. Also included in the album was the ballad 'Is This The World We Created?', the track which Mercury and May performed at Live Aid.

The next year Queen released their *Complete Works*, which proved an indispensable collection of all their albums to date, along with a special mini-album entitled *Complete Vision*. Tracks on that were the festive hit 'Thank God It's Christmas' and the flip sides to 'Seven Seas of Rhye' and 'Radio GaGa', 'See What A Fool I've Been' and 'I Go Crazy'.

One year on saw the band exceeding their previous album sales yet again with *A Kind Of Magic*, the majority of the tracks on which were written for the swashbuckling epic *Highlander*. The album rocketed to the top spot and the singles from it became big sellers all over the world. 'One Vision', Queen's tribute to Live Aid initiator Bob Geldof reached number seven, while 'A Kind Of Magic' reached number three in an eleven-week run in the charts. Both songs showed what a breadth of range Queen now encompassed: 'One Vision' was a straightforward rock song while the other was an endearing, laid-back piece of whimsy.

Other highlights on the album were 'Princes Of The Universe', the haunting ballad 'Who Wants To Live Forever?' and 'Don't Lose Your Head', featuring the vocal talents of Joan Armatrading.

After *A Kind Of Magic* the band did not produce any new material until 1989, when *The Miracle* was released. Though critics described *The Miracle* album as lacklustre it did reach number one. The album was released on 22 May 1989. Aside from 'The Invisible Man', the album was rather predictable Queen, showing little musical progression. Two singles made the top ten, 'I Want It All' and 'Breakthru'. Nevertheless, the album, which also includes the single 'The Miracle' and a rather moving song called 'Was It Worth It?', once again became a massive seller, proving the immense loyalty of Queen fans everywhere.

In 1989 the BBC dug deep in their archives and released *Queen At The Beeb*, eight tracks taken from the band's session at the corporation's studios in 1973. While it provided interesting listening for Queen fans, it lacked wide appeal.

Queen's last studio album was *Innuendo*, released in February 1991, nine months before Mercury's death. Musically, it was very much a return to form, providing some superb songs, made all the more poignant when the world realized the suffering that Mercury had been going through during its making. The title track was the first Queen song to go straight into the charts at number one. Lasting over six minutes, it became the third-longest number one (in duration) to top the UK charts and was a delightful melange of three different sections, reminiscent of the band's classic 'Bohemian Rhapsody'.

'I'm Going Slightly Mad', the second single, proved

another radical departure from the normal Queen sound, especially in its off-the-wall and amusing lyrics, which had Mercury declaring that he was 'one card short of a full deck'. But there was plenty of hard-edged rock too with 'The Hitman', 'Headlong' and 'I Can't Live With You' all showing the band in strong form. The jewels in the album's crown were 'Bijou', featuring some breathtaking guitar, and 'These Are The Days Of Our Lives', a poignant track in which Mercury reminisces about his life and his inability to turn back the clock. (The song later appeared on the double A-side number one single with 'Bohemian Rhapsody', released as a tribute to the singer.) *Innuendo* was the last studio album released before Mercury's death. The video shows a gaunt and ill-looking Mercury, his clothes hanging off him, his face like a death mask. But the record was alive with the kind of magic that was for ever Queen.

Chapter 4

THE ULTIMATE SHOWMAN

On Stage and on Film

'I love the Queen.
She does outrageous things too'

It was a quiet, discreet bash by Freddie Mercury's standards. Twelve topless waitresses bearing magnums of champagne passed among the well wishers who had come backstage to congratulate Queen on their sell-out show at New York's Madison Square Gardens. Mercury and his band were planning a proper party later on, but for the time being this modest little number would have to do.

I was having a brief taste of what it was like to be part of the court that surrounded King Freddie wherever he went. Just hours before I had been collected by a white stretch limousine, the size of a suburban bungalow, from JFK airport and whisked off to my hotel to freshen up before my audience with rock's master showman.

But though Mercury was pop's most flamboyant character, a star who made Elton John look like a shy wallflower, when it came to revealing talks he was as open as a clenched fist; in the few interviews he gave he was a master of the flippant remark, but baring his soul was never part of his make-up. But, for whatever reason, this occasion was different and I came away with one of the most intimate interviews I had ever done with a pop star.

The singer, dressed in white singlet with a plastic beaker of champagne in one hand and a king-size, filter-tipped cigarette in the other was in a relaxed and happy mood as he told me how he believed in living life to the very hilt. Leaning forward conspiratorially, his big brown eyes flickering with glee, he told me: 'Excess is part of my nature. To me dullness is a disease. I really need danger and excitement. I was not made for staying indoors and watching television. I am definitely a sexual person. I like to f*** all the time. I used to say that I would go with anyone, but these days I have become much more choosy.

'I love to surround myself with strange and interesting people because they make me feel more alive. Extremely straight people bore me stiff. I love freaky people around me.

'By nature I'm restless and highly strung, so I wouldn't make a good family man. Deep down inside I am a very emotional person, a person of real extremes and often that's destructive both to myself and others.' It was Mercury owning up to his wild side – a side that his fame and wealth allowed him to indulge in as much as he wanted, a side that he usually kept hidden behind sarcastic one-liners or bitchy put-downs. Off stage, in private, he was as emotional as he was in performance. And tonight he wasn't scared to admit it.

He put down his plastic cup and a topless waitress rushed to fill it. Waving a wonderfully limp wrist in the air he carried on hardly stopping for breath, his words pirouetting out of his mouth. 'When I have a relationship, it is never a half-hearted one. I don't believe in half measures or compromise. I just can't bear to compromise about anything. I give everything that I've got – because that's the way I am.'

When I asked him about some of the wild exotic clubs he liked to frequent he let out a high-pitched laugh. 'I love the clubs in New York. I remember once I wanted to go to a club called The Gilded Grape which I heard was really exciting, but everyone told me I shouldn't go to. Or if I did, at least to make sure I had a fast bullet-proof car waiting for me outside. Everyone trying to warn me against this club made me even more determined to go.'

Somehow Mercury managed to rope in a most unlikely companion – ex-Wimbledon tennis champion Billie-Jean King to go down there with him. 'Not long after we got there a massive fight broke out which ended up at our table. Chairs were being smashed, fists were flying there was blood everywhere. Billie was petrified, but I loved it. I told her not to worry, and as the fight raged I grabbed her and took her onto the dance floor.

'It was much more fun than having some cosy dinner back at my hotel.

'Life is for living. Believe me, I would be doing those things and having that philosophy even if I wasn't successful.'

Mercury was stopped in full flow when I asked him if there was anything the man who had everything still wanted. In a moment of pure drama Mercury, ever the performer, looked up at me with eyes that now looked soft and soulful, paused for what seemed like an eternity and said: 'Happiness. I don't think I've got that.'

He could be bold and bombastic one minute, fragile and feeling the next. On stage Freddie Mercury ran the gamut of emotions and the audience ran with him. As David Bowie, another performer with perfect stagecraft, put it, 'He was a star who could hold the audience in the palm of his hand.' When it came to stage charisma, Mercury had cornered the market and the band's shows were live musical theatre at its best.

Mercury once told me: 'To me playing in front of a big crowd – that kind of surge – is unequalled. When I go off it takes me hours to unwind and transform back into my own character.' And, it would take the crowd hours to unwind too. At a Queen concert Mercury would work tirelessly and passionately until he felt he had captured every member of the audience, and it was a wonderful sight as thousands of fans sang and swayed in unison to 'Crazy Little Thing Called Love' or 'Radio GaGa'. His performances could mesmerise crowds all over the world – though Mercury himself preferred the word 'communicate'.

In Rio, during the moving 'Love Of My Life', the 350,000-strong crowd sang along with him like a passionate, massed choir. In Montreal, where the singer stomped around the stage wearing just a pair of white shorts and a white peaked hat, they danced wildly to 'Another One Bites The Dust'.

Mercury's performances were full of dramatic gestures and he enjoyed playing a rock version of Sir Laurence Olivier to the hilt. He would toss his head back, stand legs akimbo and place his hands majestically on his hips as the music swirled around him. Or he would surge across the stage, strutting and preening like a peacock force-fed on cocaine. At other times he would brandish his sawn-off microphone stand like a rock weapon, pointing it up to the heavens, arching it behind his back in James Dean's famous rifle pose, or playing it with maniacally darting fingers as if it were a Statocaster.

Then of course there were the outfits, the like of which the rock world had never seen before – the satin catsuits with their plunging necklines revealing a forest of chest hair, the fur coats and velvet trousers and the short bolero jackets, tights and ballet pumps. 'Anything goes,' said Mercury. 'Why, Nijinsky once wore a costume made out of the finest gauze. I don't do it to shock people, it's just theatre. I like a nice frock.'

At the free concert Queen gave in London's Hyde Park in September 1976 Mercury flounced on stage in front of 150,000 fans with thickly lacquered black nail polish and a dazzling silver jump suit slit to the waist. In New York's Madison Square Gardens in February 1977 the crowd went ape as Mercury closed the show with a striptease finale of 'Hey Big Spender', waltzing out of his leotard to reveal a pair of tiny, candy-striped shorts.

Some of the most spectacular shows the band ever did were in South America, where they were the first major rock band to take the continent by storm. During a series of eight outdoor concerts in Brazil and Argentina in March 1981 Queen braved new territory and gave fans starved of live music a regal display of rock. In Argentina the whole stadium erupted when Mercury came on stage in a pair of skimpy shorts just as the Argentinian flag was slowly being raised alongside the Union Jack. He said afterwards: 'They consider it indecent for men to wear shorts, but I wanted to give them a treat. If I had worn them on the street I would have been arrested.' This was regardless of the unrest in Argentina at the time and despite the fact that everyone had been given a sheet listing things they could and could not do while they were there.

Queen's show is lavish by any standards, so in Argentina it had the audience pop-eyed with amazement. 'We once saw a film of an Argentinian band,' Mercury recalled. 'They had just a couple of amps and four lights pointed at them. We wanted to show them what a show could really be like. We wanted it to be a first not just for us, but for them too.'

The band also managed to woo eighty thousand fans in Hungary when, in 1986, they made history as the first major rock band to play behind the Iron Curtain. With Western acts still frowned upon, it was a massive step for both the band and the Hungarian people. An incredible 250,000 tickets had been applied for by Eastern bloc fans desperate to hear the band. In Budapest he and the crowd united to sing a traditional Hungarian song Tavaski Szel. Mercury reading the words from the palm of his hand to make sure it was perfect. The crowd loved the gesture and took him to their hearts and the stadium erupted with cheers and rapturous applause. Some fans in the front rows got so carried away the authorities had to drench them with buckets of water to cool them down.

Denis O' Regan was the band's official photographer on that tour. 'I really liked working with the band,' he said. 'They were all fun and very professional. And of course Freddie was a real one-off. He could be wonderfully grand and so larger than life. I remember one time we were in Germany when we were all up in Freddie's room. We had all come back from a show and we had decided to watch some footabll on the TV. By the time it had finished all the limousines had been sent away and there was a bit of fussing around trying to find some transport to take us to a local club. When I asked Freddie if they had finally managed to get something to travel in, he looked at me and very grandly said: 'Yes we have, dear boy, I believe we are going in something that is called a cab.'

Regan also remembers how when the band played Budapest, Mercury managed to get the sumptious Presidential suite in the city's top hotel – which was only given to heads of state and royalty. 'It was so enormous and opulent that all the other band members came up to the room to have a look at it. As they were gazing around Freddie told them: "All suites are equal, though some are more equal than others," to which Roger retorted: "Well, it's a f*** sight more equal than mine".'

Queen's 'Magic' tour in 1986 was the most electric and elaborate the band ever did. Over one million people saw the band during the tour which went all over Europe, and in excess of four hundred thousand saw them in Britain alone. There were twenty-six dates in all. Mercury was at his majestic best, sporting the full regalia of an English monarch– deep ruby-red robe, trimmed with ermine, and jewel-encrusted crown. Queen's designer Diane Moseley said th   e cloak weighed twenty pounds and was made up of fourteen metres of red velvet trimmed with fur, ermine skins and bullion gold, all lined with red silk. Moseley described it as a 'Napoleonic coronation robe', and it was said to have cost £1,500.

In Germany, at Mannheim's Sports Park, in June

1986, that year Mercury proved he was a true rock king, whose adoring subjects obeyed his every whim, when, brandishing a sceptre as his baton, he conducted eighty thousand Germans in a guttural rendition of the British national anthem. When the show got to Britain there were more spectacular effects. At Wembley, Mercury, dressed as an Olympic athlete, ascended two flights of stairs to light giant torches while massive blow-up dolls filled with helium floated high above the stadium.

Despite Queen's reputation for putting on outstanding live shows, tours did not always go according to plan. The band's debut jaunt through the States in 1974 had to be cancelled after only a few nights when Brian May came down with hepatitis. 'Our plans were totally wrecked,' Brian recalls. 'We had to quit the tour with another month of dates outstanding. We flew home and I had to go to bed and stay there.' Disaster struck again when Queen toured America the next year. This time Mercury was taken ill halfway through the tour with suspected throat nodules. (Voice troubles were something that Mercury often suffered from, as he would sing his heart out, no matter what the show.) As a result seven concerts were cancelled before he managed to recover and the band hit the road again.

Some shows never even got off the ground. In 1982 Queen were reported to have been forced to scrap two huge planned shows – one at Manchester United's football ground, the other at Arsenal's – because of toilet troubles. As a result of Pope John Paul II's first visit to Britain, all the available portable toilets had apparently been installed in the various cities on his route, and there were none left.

Although Queen were the most a-political of bands and preached none of the messages of revolution that fired so many other rock groups, they found themselves in scalding political water over a series of dates in South Africa in 1984. The band took a nasty hammering after they played Sun City, a lush resort in Bophuthatswana, and what was dubbed the country's answer to Las Vegas. Mercury was reported to have said that 'there was a lot of money to be made there', and Queen were roundly rebuked and put on a United Nations blacklist for not honouring the cultural boycott. In Britain the Musicians' Union suspended the group despite their protestations that they were totally against apartheid and saw the dates as bridge-building exercises. In the end the band appealed against the decision. It was overturned and they escaped with a £2,000 fine. But the South African shows sullied their image among many rock fans with liberal, idealistic leanings, despite Queen's repeated protests that they felt they had done nothing wrong. Brian May later hit out, saying: 'The only criticism we got was from outside South Africa.' Trouble struck again during the tour when fans were left furious after Mercury lost his voice at one of the Sun City shows, where the band were due to perform before seven thousand people, and the concert had to be scrapped as a result.

And sometimes Queen found themselves in the wars through the silliest of pranks. That was the case when Mercury pranced on stage in full drag – complete with inflatable bosoms, tight-fitting women's clothes and a wig – in front of 325,000 fans at the 1985 Rock in Rio show. As Mercury launched into Queen's huge hit of the previous year, 'I Want To Break Free', the video of which had seen all the members camping it up in various states of cross-dressing, the audience launched into him, pelting him with stones. A shocked and upset Mercury had not realized that South American fans cherished this song, above all the band's others, because they saw in its lyrics a potent political message of freedom – a freedom which they were so desperately fighting to achieve under a brutal and repressive regime. But as the missiles hurled down on him, Mercury, ever quick, realized that it was his tranvestism which had provoked their rage and did the fastest striptease his fans were ever to see, ripping off his wig and false bust, and calming the audience in an instant. Afterwards, though upset, he was able to laugh off the incident in his usual self-deprecating way, saying that another great queen had once been stoned too – the Queen of Sheba.

Queen were like a marriage and like any marriage were prone to almighty rows and threats of divorce. Publicised bust-ups and rumours that the band were on the verge of splitting up plagued them throughout their career. But despite the rows, the tantrums and the ultimatums the group stuck it out together. When Mercury died the four of them had been together for twenty years.

It was never going to be a docile partnership: all four members of the band were independent, strong-willed, and knew what they wanted. And they stuck to their guns. For if Mercury was Queen's most outrageous and outspoken member and the driving force of the band, it appeared that none of the others was content to take a back seat and let him run the show. The rows could be about anything – from the guitar playing in a song to someone's hair – and the arguments were often as hot as a geyser in full spurt.

Mercury himself once told me: 'I'm a very emotional musician and not the easiest person to get along with. And that creates a lot of problems within the band. Tempers will and do flare. I can be volatile and difficult. But then I am a perfectionist. I don't see the point of not being one when it comes to our music. Being second-best has never interested me. Queen are capable of great things, but sometimes great things take great courage.' And he added: 'There have been times when we have hated each others' guts. There have been times when I just needed half a year off and took it. Times when I found everything too formulated and too rigid. The life of a rock band is to go into the studio, make an album, go out on the road and then start the whole thing all over again. I had enough and I wanted to break free. I believe you should never get trapped in a rut and if you feel you are in one you should get out. I love the music we make. I am passionate about it, but I also believe life is about other things – sometimes I just want to go shopping, clubbing and just having a ball.'

But Mercury wasn't the only wilful one. All the band were strong characters who wanted, and got, a say in the running of what started off just as a small group and then exploded into a business organisation with a Midas touch. 'One of our biggest problems is having four such strong, independent personalities,' Mercury once said. And the band's one-time American publicist Bryn Bridenthal acknowledged: 'There were volatile times, but that was part of what made the magic. The band were four very distinctive personalities, and whenever you have such distinct personalities working as a unit, there is going to be drama. But I think all that contributed to the whole, it contributed to the success. I think the "tiffs" or whatever you want to call them contributed to the success. Despite it all, the band were always great friends and had great respect for one another.'

Even back in 1977, just three years after the band first hit the charts with 'Seven Seas of Rhye', it was apparent that the group were a temperamental force, with Taylor conceding: 'Our rows are partially a conflict of musical ideas and partially ego problems.' And those pressures intensified as the band became more successful, embarked on longer and more gruelling tours and spent more time locked up in recording studios trying to better their last record. Their constant striving for perfection meant that even when it came to choosing a 'Greatest Hits' collection there would be rows about which songs to include and which to leave out in the cold.

At times the pop world held its breath and wondered if the rows would cause the band to implode. Mercury declared: 'The rumours that Queen are splitting up are always doing the rounds. Some people just seem to want us to break up. Heaven knows why. Yes, there are a lot of tensions and stresses in the band and sometimes we have the most almighty rows, but they just clear the air.

'It isn't true to say we always row. Let's just say there's a degree of tension which often pushes us into sticky situations. But once we've got down to the business of making music, everything else is forgotten. Besides I would rather we had the occasional almighty blow-up than days of sulking and not speaking to one another, which is so counterproductive. The rows can be fierce, but at least they iron out any problems and each of us knows where he stands.

'We don't hate each other. If we did it would be a different matter, but the reverse is true. Our blow-outs happen because we become jaded. It can be draining and uninspiring working as hard as we do and you constantly have to be on your guard to stop things becoming monotonous. There was a time, for instance, when all our tours seemed to be in the winter, and I wanted to break that. I just thought for fuck's sake, let's do a summer tour. Let's do something different.'

May affirmed: 'During the worst time we weren't even talking to each other. There was a real problem. Being in a group is just like being married in a way, only more difficult. You haven't got just one partner to deal with but three, who are all pulling different ways, who all have different opinions,' John Deacon, for his part, remembers that there were heated differences of opinion about whether the majestic song he wrote, 'Another One Bites The Dust', should come out as a single. Eventually the band released it and it became one of their biggest hits. But they rowed so much about what records to include on albums that just before *The Works* came out they agreed to the peace-keeping solution that the album would feature three songs each from Mercury and May and two each from Taylor and Deacon.

In a revealing interview with America's prestigious *Rolling Stone* magazine, Deacon, the band's softly spoken bass player, admitted that Mercury's flamboyantly vulgar image often annoyed and irritated the other group members: 'Some of us hate it, but that's Freddie and you can't stop it. Like one time he did an interview and said things like "We're dripping with money, darling."'

As a result of the continuing rows rumours of a split abounded in the pop world. They came to a head when Mercury did his debut solo album, *Mr Bad Guy*, released in 1985, in Munich. But Mercury denied them, claiming that the band were just taking a break from each other to pursue different projects: 'There were still lots of styles I wanted to do with Queen but I wasn't able to. Not that Queen can't do them; we just haven't. This album gave me the chance to use a live orchestra, which I always wanted to do with Queen but never succeeded because Brian does an orchestra with his guitar.'

More rumours that the band were parting company blew up when Mercury said he thought he was too old for touring and that he was sick of the gruelling work involved in continually going on the road: 'I don't think a forty-two-year-old man should be running around in his leotard any more. It's not very becoming.' As it became evident that Queen seemed unlikely to tour – their last outing was the Magic Tour in 1986 – more rumours began to spread that the band were at loggerheads. But the truth of the matter was far sadder: Mercury was dying and a tour would have been suicide.

The group stayed 'married' till the end – loyal to each other – and it was only death that separated them. Years before, in a documentary video, Mercury remarked: 'I think the reason we have stayed together so long is that none of us wants to leave. If you leave it's like you are a coward. We still keep going. As long as people keep buying the music then it's OK. When they stop buying our records then I'll say goodbye and do something else, like become a strip artist!' But the records wouldn't stop selling, the fans stayed patiently faithful and Mercury never did pursue a striptease career.

Queen's videos were, for the most part, a feast of fun and fantasy, every bit as entertaining and over-the-top as their live performances. But then the band had a lot to live up to as the pioneers of pop video with their ground-breaking *Bohemian Rhapsody* film way back in 1975.

The videos gave the band, especially Mercury, a chance to be as visually imaginative as possible, even if it meant sending themselves up mercilessly. Mercury and the band never became pompous, the way so many rock stars do with the advent of fame and fortune.

One of their most memorable videos was for John Deacon's song 'I Want To Break Free', where the whole group dressed in drag, looking like the inmates of British TV's longest-running soap opera, 'Coronation Street'. Mercury donned a pair of huge false breasts and squeezed his bulging torso into a pink jumper and his skinny legs into a black mini-skirt. The video shows him flaunting himself in a dusty living room, hoover in hand, while Brian May lounges on a settee with his wild curly hair tightly packed under a head of rollers.

In that 1984 video, which cost more than £100,000 to make, Mercury went from one extreme to another, appearing at one stage as Nijinsky's fawn, complete with long painted ears and body stocking. His famous moustache was even removed for the scene where he poses on top of a rock playing a set of pipes. The video also features members of the Royal Ballet, who roll the singer over their taut bodies, sensuously moving him into balletic poses.

Wayne Eagling, the choreographer of *I Want To Break Free*, recalls Mercury as a consummate professional when it came to making videos: 'Freddie had this image of Nijinsky's fawn which he wanted to recreate on stage, with him playing pipes and sitting on a rock. It took a lot of practice, especially the piece when he rolls down on the other dancers, but he was very game.

'He was easy to work with and put a lot of effort into everything he did. He always came into rehearsals wearing tights. He was the ultimate professional.'

In all the group's videos Mercury always created the precise image he wanted in order to capture fully the spirit and lyrics of each individual song. At times he felt it was appropriate simply to do what he excelled at, which was performing as the band's flamboyant front man before an adoring audience. For example, Queen recreated a typical concert scene with the help of a thousand fans for their 1986 video *Friends Will Be Friends*. At one point Mercury stands twenty-five feet above the crowd on a mobile crane, which projects a beam of white light on the sea of faces below. The video reached its climax when Mercury strutted on stage in a white jump suit and conducted the crowd as they sang the tender chorus.

Occasionally videos would feature all kinds of archive footage intercut with shots of Mercury cavorting on stage. *Radio GaGa* includes war scenes and footage from one of the landmarks of film history, *Metropolis*, interspersed with scenes of the band. Dressed in striking red tops and black trousers, the band orders the audience to punch their arms in the air to the hypnotic chant of 'Radio GaGa'.

Mercury and the band approached their videos in the same way as their music; they were perfectionists determined never to mine the same seam. Mercury's friend Dave Clark said: 'When you look at a lot of his videos he knew just how to depict what was said in the lyrics. He knew exactly what he wanted, right down to the look and the lighting of the whole thing.' Queen were always eager to experiment with all sorts of visual tricks, such as the use of animation. In the 1986 video for *It's A Kind Of Magic* Mercury appeared as a magician dressed in a sweeping black cloak and hat. As if by magic he conjured up three animated dancers and later extinguished them with a sparkle of magic dust. The use of visual tricks reached its peak in the 1991 *Innuendo*, when the band members were themselves recreated as animated characters. When it came to choosing the venues, wardrobe and props the sky was the limit. Mercury loved to dress up and create superb sets fit for the grandest theatre, opera or ballet. Anything was permitted, provided it was larger than life.

No expense was spared for Queen's 1984 video *It's A Hard Life*, which was shot over two days in Munich and featured one of Mercury's closest friends, Barbara Valentin. The singer was decked out in an elaborate scarlet costume decorated with ostrich feathers and huge eyes. The medieval set was designed and built in two days and included a banquet hall complete with marble pillars, balcony and golden trelliswork. Drummer Roger Taylor commented: 'It's what you might call a typical Queen production. We believe if a thing's worth doing it's worth doing well.'

The rock band fully exploited the video medium

to show off Mercury's outrageous theatrical performances and ornate costumes. In front of a camera
Mercury was always prepared to ham it up, whether
that meant dressing in drag or cavorting with classical
dancers. Behind the camera the singer's training in
graphic design and strong visual sense combined to
make Queen one of the leaders in the pop video
field. 'We realized earlier on there was a different
way to sell records and now video has become an
integral part of making music,' Mercury said. 'When
you release a single it conjures up an image and videos
can make that image come to life. Besides a group can't
be everywhere at the same time, but a video can.'

Elton John recognized that Queen were the over-
lords of the pop video. In a BBC TV tribute to the star,
he said: 'Queen were the band who really started off
videos. In this, as in many other aspects, they were
innovative. They had all the great ideas to start with.'
'Bohemian Rhapsody' was the record which started
the video revolution. Of the promo film, which began
with the band's four faces cloaked in shadow, Mercury
was later to say: 'That was our first lavish production,
even though then we didn't have much money to
spend and had to do everything ourselves.'

As the band became increasingly successful they
spent more and more money on lavish video productions – though they did not always work out. In
1985 a video of the singer's black and white costumed
birthday ball held at a Munich nightclub was banned
by CBS, the company for whom he was making his
solo album, as 'too dangerous'. The video to promote
Mercury's single 'Living On My Own' cost £30,000 to
make and featured friends of the rock star dressed
in drag. But music chiefs at CBS were scared of the

public's reaction to such camp behaviour. At the time a spokesman for CBS said: 'We believe this video could be seen as being in bad taste.'

Queen's 1982 *Body Language* was also banned by numerous television shows because it was considered too raunchy. The stylish video, which was set in a Turkish bath, featured a leather-clad Mercury surrounded by sensuously writhing dancers. Director Mike Hodges recalled: 'There was a lot of writhing and gyrating in the video, though I thought it was rather tame.'

One of the band's most lavish videos was *Who Wants To Live For Ever?*, which cost around £150,000 and featured the National Philharmonic Orchestra and forty choirboys. It was shot in a huge tobacco warehouse in London's East End with Mercury looking dapper in a hand-stitched suit and white silk tie. One of the most daring was their 1989 video *Breakthru*, prior to which the band insured themselves for about £2 million against serious injury. For the £200,000 video the group were filmed playing live in an open-top express train carriage hurtling along at sixty mph. At the time a Queen spokesman said: 'The band felt it was wise to take out a substantial insurance policy for what could be an extremely dangerous filming session.' The video showed how meticulously they had worked, even hand-painting individual lumps of coal.

For their *Miracle* video the band auditioned for children who bore a resemblance to how the four of them had looked during their schooldays. Mercury watched his young 'self' strut around the stage in his customized black and white body leotard and black PVC jacket and exclaimed: 'The resemblance was quite frightening.'

As AIDS took its toll Mercury battled bravely to keep making the videos he loved doing so much. For the film to accompany 'I'm Going Slightly Mad' he disguised himself heavily with long black wig and theatrical white make-up so that fans would not see how ill he looked. For others, like *Innuendo*, he didn't make an appearance, while *The Show Must Go On* featured the band as animated characters plus old footage.

The last 'real' video Mercury made was for 'I'm Going Slightly Mad', but Queen did shoot one more film for the posthumously released 'These Are The Days Of Our Lives'. It was shot in black and white and features a gaunt, ill-looking Mercury singing delicately to the camera. There are no visual pyrotechnics, no colourful scenes, no outrageous behaviour. Unlike past Queen videos, this one has nothing lavish, opulent or frivolous about it. But it was the most moving promotional film they ever shot.

Chapter 5

ADVENTURES IN GERMANY

Behind the Scenes in Munich

'I am the manipulator of my life'

Freddie Mercury looked like a million dollars in his scarlet catsuit emblazoned with huge green eyes and slashed dramatically to show a huge expanse of hairy chest. He was preparing to dazzle yet another audience and checked his appearance in the mirror to make sure it was perfect. It was. But that didn't stop the huge surge of stage fright which suddenly paralysed his whole body. 'I can go out there. I can go out there. I can go out there,' he kept on repeating to himself as he psyched himself up for his performance. His stage fright would have been understandable if he'd been facing an audience of a hundred thousand, but Mercury was changing in a small Munich bedroom for a children's birthday party attended by about twenty infants.

'It might seem unbelievable, but it was true,' says Reinhold Mack, the first producer after Roy Thomas Baker to work with the band. 'At times Freddie could be exceptionally shy and often he was scared shitless if he was in a room full of people. I remember the time he got "stage fright" in my bedroom so well. My eldest son had a birthday around the time the band were doing recordings for *Hot Space* and Freddie said he was going to turn up in his red eye costume because it would be such a surprise and thrill for the kids. He was as good as his word, too, even though I realized what an ordeal it was going to be for him. When I went into the bedroom to see how he was getting on with his changing, there he was in the middle of the room psyching himself up and repeating: "I can do it" over and over to himself. And of course he could, although he wasn't even going to sing for them. All he was doing was just parading around in that wonderful costume and talking to the children. They thought it was incredible, and it was. I bet there weren't many better children's parties than that one.'

This wasn't an isolated incidence of Mercury's shyness. Despite having one of the best voices in the rock world, there were times when he was even shy of singing. One such occasion was in a small village church in Germany. Mack recalls: 'During the christening of my youngest son, John Frederick [John Deacon and Freddie were the little boy's godparents], my oldest son Julian was standing next to Freddie during the singing and noticed that Freddie wasn't singing. Julian couldn't understand why such a world-famous artist, who could hold thousands of people spellbound with his voice, wasn't singing. He began hitting him, saying: "Come on, sing! Everybody is singing, and you're a singer." But Freddie wouldn't. It might seem strange, but then one thing that people really don't realise about Freddie is what a modest man he was.'

Mercury met Mack in 1979 when Queen decided

to work at one of Munich's most famous studios, The Musicland, where legendary producer Giorgio Moroder composed some of his greatest hits and changed the face of disco. Mercury fell in love with the town immediately and began spending more and more time there. He even made it his home for two years, and it was in Munich that he made some of his closest friends and had some of the most fun times of his life.

Like New York, where Mercury also bought a flat, Munich was a mecca for homosexual culture and gay bars and Mercury loved its easy-going atmosphere and the fact that he could do as he wanted there without fear of criticism or censorship. It was in Munich that he could finally be himself. The town had a bustling and lively gay area called the Bermuda Triangle, and Mercury was a regular there, visiting its numerous clubs, including New York, Frisco and the Ochsen Gardens. 'He came to Munich an awful lot,' Mack recalls, 'and lived there continuously at one period for almost two years. I think one of the reasons he liked it there so much was because the gay scene was far more open and relaxed there than most other places in the world.

'The bars there were such fun, much more fun than the city's straight bars. They were frivolous, noisy and packed with people. And they didn't just attract gay people – straight men would go down there, as would girls. Freddie loved to be around a real mix of people. He never liked the purely gay world.'

Freddie went to Munich with various colleagues, and people who were indispensable to him, including his personal manager, Paul Prenter, Peter Freestone and Joe Fannelli. 'Phoebe [Peter Freestone] and Joe

[Joe Fannelli] came with him to make his life more comfortable,' says Mack. 'They were employed by Freddie to do all those everyday things like look after the clothes, cook and just keep things going. But at the same time it was never really felt they were employees. They were Freddie's good friends as much as anything else.' It was in Munich that the band were to record some of their adventurous music.

Despite Mercury's homosexual promiscuity – which Munich was the perfect place to indulge – a number of his friends believe that he found his gay life ultimately dissatisfying. Mack himself believed that the singer planned eventually to give it up and even get married and start a family. It was not an impossible dream – after all, Mercury had lived with Mary Austin for seven years and at one point the two were contemplating marriage. Mack believes that Mercury would have loved a family of his own – a desire that had its roots in his childhood, when he was often away from his parents for long stretches at a time. Speaking to me from his Munich flat, he said: 'Freddie told me a number of times: "Perhaps I'll give up the whole gay thing one of these days." I didn't think that was strange at all. He more or less decided when he was twenty-four or twenty-five that he was gay and before that he was considered as straight. With him nothing was impossible. I do think he could have given up being gay, because he loved women. I saw what he was like in their presence and he wasn't the kind of gay man who didn't like them in his life. He was the opposite.'

Queen's former record producer realized how much Mercury thought about having a family whenever Mercury made one of his frequent visits to see him and his wife and children at their Munich home: 'Freddie's biggest thing was to have a family and a normal life. I had a problem about five years ago when I got badly screwed by an accountant and I had to pay lots of back tax. I was discussing my problem with Freddie one day and said I couldn't deal with it all. He told me: "Fuck, it's only money! Why worry about something like that? You've got it made, you've got everything you need – a wonderful family and children. You have everything I can never have." That's when I became aware that when he was at our house he was watching everything and taking it all in and seeing what a family life was like and how it could have made him happy. My own family is a very close one.

'I believe Freddie would have liked a family very, very much. He was very sentimental in many ways. His close relationship with Mary carried on until the end, maybe because he felt guilty at never marrying her, and everybody who was close to him was treated as part of a family to some extent.

'Freddie didn't have a real close family around him when he was growing up from what I learned. He liked my second boy, Felix, the best because he was very artistic. One day I overheard a conversation between them when they were both sitting on the couch together. Freddie was telling Felix: 'I never had any of this. When I was young I spent a lot of time away from my parents because I was at boarding school. Sometimes I would hardly ever see them.

'He had quite a hard time as a child. Especially when he came over to London at such a difficult age, in his early teens. If you come from a strange, exotic country and look very different from the other kids you are going to get bullied and have a tough time, especially somewhere like London.

'He talked to my kids about his childhood quite a lot. But then Freddie adored children. As soon as children could walk and talk and respond he got on with them.'

In Munich Mercury fell in love with a handsome German restaurateur called Winnie, who was similar in looks to Mercury's last ever boyfriend, Jim Hutton. The couple met at one of Munich's many gay bars and their relationship lasted for much of Mercury's stay in the Bavarian town. 'I think one of the things that attracted Freddie to Winnie was that when they first met Winnie didn't know who Freddie was and after he was told really didn't care,' Mack recalls. 'He wasn't impressed by Freddie's fabulous wealth, at the beginning, either. When Freddie once told him he had a car and driver waiting outside the club for them, Winnie told him: "I don't give a s***. I'm walking and if you want to be with me, you'll walk as well." Freddie found that all so refreshing. Like a lot of big stars he liked the idea of someone liking him just for himself and not for who he was.'

Mercury and Winnie, a former bartender, were very much in love, despite Freddie's promiscuity and the fact that the Munich bars were packed with legions of gay men who had the 'butch, lorry driver's' looks to which Mercury was so susceptible. 'Freddie loved the idea of having a steady relationship,' Mack recalls, 'but if he wasn't involved in one he was promiscuous. When he was in a loving relationship, he was often "straighter" than a straight person. Freddie was very domesticated. I remember how he loved helping

Winnie put the chairs up in his restaurant and vacuum the whole place to make it spotless. He quite openly admitted that when he went home he was a boring person. Freddie was never boring, but what he meant was that he loved home life. He was concerned about how the pictures looked in a room and if they were hanging right or how his garden and his flowers were doing. He was very domesticated. And when he was in Munich he loved to go shopping for things to decorate his home. He and my wife would go shopping together. He bought lots of paintings, porcelain and china here.

'Freddie loved being in love. He was a quick song-writer and composer at the best of times, but when he was in love he wrote all the faster. If he was depressed he really wouldn't write anything and consequently there are really no depressing Queen songs. Even his moving ballads weren't depressing. And though a lot of people have talked about the haunting lyrics in the "Show Must Go On", I think that is a very positive and optimistic song.'

Of Freddie's gayness, Mack says: 'Freddie wasn't one to broadcast about his sex life. He was quite a private person, but at the same time he was open about it here. The men who most turned him on were strong, builder types. I don't know why. I once told him: You should go for someone a bit more in your class than a bricklayer.' But he obviously didn't agree.

'Unlike some gays, Freddie didn't put the whole gay thing right into your face. When there were other people around he was very careful about their feelings. I really respected him for that. For instance, when he was in restaurants with a lot of other people who weren't gay he was never outrageous. He was always very conscious about not offending anyone.'

Towards the end of his relationship with Winnie, Mercury fell in love with a former hairdresser called Jim Hutton. 'Winnie was very obviously jealous about Jim and did a couple of horrible things which upset Freddie,' Mack recalls. 'Freddie had given Winnie a beautiful Mercedes 560 and Winnie sold it. He also sold a wonderful piano that Freddie had in the apartment.' Mercury would have regarded sales of things like that as a betrayal and when he decided to leave Munich and go back to Kensington to live in his new home, which workmen had been in the process of totally rebuilding and decorating for the last five years, he left Winnie behind. He set up home in his Kensington 'palace' with Jim, who was to be the last boyfriend in his life.

Mercury's former personal manager, Paul Prenter, who broke with Mercury after working for him for nine years and then sold his story about life with the singer, was a vital part of the Munich scene. 'I got on well with Paul, but he was a shady character,' says Mack. 'He was always taking advantage of Freddie in all kinds of ways – from money to drugs. He would take a gram of cocaine, hoping Freddie wouldn't notice, and Freddie never did. And I remember another time he said he was mugged on the street and two thousand dollars was stolen. That was very suspicious. No one else got mugged here, or no one else lost money; it was always him.

'I actually think Paul was more overpowering and more outrageous than Freddie. It was as if he was always trying to outdo him and in the end he just went too far and went out of control.'

Mack was another of the select group who enjoyed Mercury's lavish parties, especially his birthday ones.

There was ten days' age difference between them. 'I loved his parties,' he says. 'My wife decorated his black and white birthday party. That was such a laugh. The men all had to wear drag. I knew Freddie loved ballet, so I wore a ballet outfit. And the hat party Freddie had in Kensington was another great bash, even if Freddie couldn't make up his mind which hat to wear. He had about ten different hats made, including one which was a very large top hat whose top would open when a string was pulled and out popped a very large penis. Another hat he had made was one that consisted of a very large fruit basket. In the end Freddie didn't wear any of them. He said he didn't want to upset the different designers who had made them by favouring one above the others.'

Mercury and Mack first ran into each other at Munich's Musicland studios, which Mack had built with Giorgio Moroder. A number of top acts had recorded at the studio, including the Rolling Stones, Deep Purple and Marc Bolan, and Queen decided to try it out. They had decided to record abroad for tax reasons, among others, and Munich seemed a better place than most they had passed through on their travels.

'We came together really by accident,' the producer says. 'The band came to the studio here in Munich. I got a mysterious message to come there and do some work. I rang up from wherever it was in the world that I happened to be at the time, but nobody seemed to know anything about the recording session. Eventually I decided to just fly there. I turned up at the studio a few minutes before Freddie arrived. He was one of the first to come in and he said: "What are you doing her?" and I said I was supposed to do the session. Freddie told me that he didn't know I was available but that it was great, and if I wanted to work with them we should start straightaway. We did "Crazy Little Thing Called Love" there and then. It was the first time Freddie had ever played rhythm guitar. He told me: "I can't play guitar, but it won't matter." I think Freddie fancied playing guitar himself for a change because he told me that he wanted to do the song real quick before Brian arrived and started putting his guitar solos on it. Freddie was looking for a different sound. I just put some rock and roll echoes on it and it sounded great.'

Mack was impressed at the lightning speed at which Mercury worked. That rock and roll pastiche with Mercury on guitar took just six hours, yet it was a huge hit all over the world, reaching number two in the British charts. 'Freddie was amazingly fast. He used to write things in about twenty minutes,' says Mack. 'I think he might have had an idea for one of the major lines for "Crazy Little Thing" before he came in, but then he just sort of made it up as he went along. It was awesome.

'I got on exceptionally well with Freddie. I liked the fact that he was a genius. He really was in terms of perception of music and seeing the focal point of where the song should be. But it wasn't just his musical talent that enthralled me. It didn't take long for me to realize what a wonderful guy he was. He was so sensitive. He was always so concerned about my life, my children and my family. And he was genuinely concerned.'

Mack brought a new dimension to the Queen sound, perfectly matching the musical mood of the time and he and the group between them came up with some prodigious sounds. One of the best disco songs ever made is 'Another One Bites The Dust': 'I think I can say that without me "Another One Bites The Dust" wouldn't exist. I put on silly noises when no one else was around to give it more of a different feel. But I don't think Queen came to Munich with a master plan of what they wanted to do. I think it just happened when we got together in the studio.'

Mack says that Mercury had a short attention span and if things went on to long he would lose interest: 'If something was laborious and long-winded he stopped it. There was never a longer period than about an hour and a half when he was really focused on something. With 'Killer Queen', you can tell that he just sat down at the piano and did it. The end is a little bit unresolved. I think that was a typical Freddie quality. He just loved to get on with something newer and more different.'

It was in Munich that Mercury had to have his leg in plaster for six weeks after snapping a tendon while he was in a nightclub. According to Mack, reports that Mercury had been involved in a club brawl were off the mark: 'There was no fight. Lots of people were larking around and someone tried to be clever and kicked him in the back of the knee. It happened when Freddie was hugging one of his friends and as he lifted him up someone came up behind him and kicked him.

'He called me very early the next morning and I knew there was trouble because normally he would never call before twelve. He was a night-time person. I took him to hospital and he had to have his leg in a cast for almost two months.'

But even when he was laid up with the injury Mercury refused to stop working and never lost his sense of humour – it was just the way he behaved when faced with a much more serious illness in years to come. 'Almost every day I would go to the apartment, pick him up, carry him to the car, sit him down in it and then drive him to the studio,' says Mack. 'I think he was very grateful that I never suggested that he should stop work because that would have just driven him crazy. Freddie loved being busy. He got bored so easily. But even with that cast on his leg he was still his jokey self. When he sat down that first day to play the piano, it proved to be somewhat difficult. He told me: "With this damned cast I can't reach the keys and the pedals at the same time. Now which one do you want me to reach?"'

Mercury was a marvellous piano player. 'I had been playing the piano far longer than Freddie,' says Mack, 'but he was in a different league to me. He could play anything and was superb at conjuring up melodies from thin air. His own musical tastes were so varied too. He liked so many things, from Aretha Franklin, who was his favourite singer, through to disco and a lot of classical music. But sitting through a whole concerto would have been too much for him – he just liked the best bits.'

Although Mercury wrote many emotional, passionate lyrics, Mack, who knew him from the first recordings in Munich in 1979 up to when Mercury left the town in 1985, felt he never let his songs become too personally revealing. 'I think there was usually a little bit of disguised personal feelings in his writing, but it was quite difficult to see because he didn't believe in writing about personal feelings or political things. He was actually quite modest about his songs, but he knew when he had written a good one. That's what

I call genius. You sit down and write something and it's so good. You don't even question it or analyse it. Often he would say: "What do you think of this?" and I would reply: "It's very good". Then he would say: "Wait a minute" and change a chord here and there. Then a big smile would come over his face as he told me: "Now it's better, isn't it?"'

In Munich Mercury did his first solo album, *Mr Bad Guy*, with Mack again in charge of production. 'The songs on *Mr Bad Guy* came very quickly, though of course this time it was all so different because there was no band. Freddie was very happy with the album. He told my wife he would let me do the next one totally and just come in and sing it. *Mr Bad Guy* is going to be re-released in September. Not all that much happened with it the first time around because the Queen fans wouldn't accept that type of music. It was very forward-looking.'

When Mercury decided to leave Munich, Mack wasn't surprised: 'His beautiful house in Kensinton had finally been finished and Freddie decided it would be silly to leave it empty and decided to move in. But I don't think when he left Munich he knew he was ill. That happened a bit later. I think that was the next year, 1986. Certainly in Ibiza in 1987 he had these spots on his face and I was a bit concerned and asked him what it was, but he just laughed it off and didn't come up with an explanation. He didn't want loads of sympathy. He believed he could fight it because he had such great reserves of strength and amazing willpower. If he wanted to do something, he could do it. He went from taking a lot of cocaine one day to taking none the next and didn't miss it at all. Freddie had great control. I think he felt he could beat his illness because, otherwise, he wouldn't have battled so bravely and lasted so long.'

Despite his failing health Mercury kept on working and thinking of new projects. 'I think one of the things he wanted to do was a big orchestral thing, which he never really got achieved,' says Mack. 'He liked putting ideas together, thinking up different ideas. His linking with Montserrat Caballé was interesting, but I don't think Montserrat's voice really complemented Freddie's at all. She could sing all the notes right but not in the way you need for rock.'

Mack doesn't believe there are lots of hidden Queen gems stockpiled away in the vaults, as some reports suggest: 'There might be one or two more albums, but there are not lots. There were never a lot of songs sitting on the side from the old sessions. And after *Barcelona* Freddie really wasn't that strong. He would only show up at the studio for a couple of hours once or twice a week as far as I know. I didn't work on *Innuendo*. I decided to go to America, but I did talk to Freddie afterwards and offered my help, but he said: "No, David Richards is doing that and besides it would take too long for you." But he always kept me up-to-date on sessions and would joke: "You really dodged the bullet. It's taken a year and we really haven't got anything together. It's just so long-winded." He wasn't really too happy about how things were going in the studio and now I know why, because he didn't have the power really. It was towards the end and his strength was ebbing away. Imagine it – one day you're able to walk and run and then all of a sudden you can't. You can't do everyday things like you used to any more.'

Mack last spoke to Mercury in July, just four months

before he died. 'Even then he was very positive,' he says. 'When I asked how he was, he told me he didn't feel bad and there was no point in grumbling. I'm sure the reason he didn't really want to see anyone towards the end was that he wanted people to remember him as he once was, healthy and fun-loving, not as a bedridden invalid. Freddie didn't feel guilty about his life. Everyone has regrets, but I think he came to terms with what was happening to him incredibly courageously.'

Chapter 6

SPEND, SPEND, SPEND

A Life style
for the Rich and Famous

*'Boredom is the biggest disease
in the whole world, darling'*

No one in the pop world threw a better party than Freddie Mercury. In an industry which seeks any excuse, no matter how trivial, to throw a bash and where celebrations cram every day of the calendar, Mercury's parties were legendary. When you went to one you never forgot it.

I went to four Mercury parties, one in Montreux, one in Munich, and two in London. The best, and one of the best bashes out of the thousands I have been to in the pop world, was the extravaganza held at London's Roof Gardens Club, just off High Street Kensington and a few minutes away from Mercury's own London home, following one of Queen's concerts at Wembley Stadium in July 1986.

It was a party that had everything – celebrities, sex and scandal. It was a party which started as soon as guests arrived in the reception area of the eight-storey

building and rode the lift to the top floor, where the
Gardens Club nestled overlooking the London skyline.
Each of the club's lifts was manned by a naked girl,
her voluptuous body daubed with paint like a walking
canvas. Inside more body-painted beauties, serving
champagne and food, mingled among the exquisitely
dressed guests. Gorgeous, semi-naked bodies were
everywhere. Even in the toilets. In the ladies' toilets
women were greeted by a muscular young blond male
dressed just in a leather jock strap and chains, while
in the gents the men were welcomed by a girl in a
sexy French maid's uniform who offered to give them
a 'massage'.

Hardened party goers who thought they had seen it
all were dazzled by the event and couldn't stop talking
about it, while photographers fought with each other
as they tried to snap pictures of the naked girls offering
their wares to the famous names in attendance. The
guest list that balmy night in July 1986 was a weird
and wonderful mixture, just the way Freddie loved
it. Being famous helped you to get an invite, but if
you were outrageous or bizarre that did the trick
too. Apart from the rest of the band, the list included
God-fearing pop star Cliff Richard, rock group Spandau
Ballet, Duran Duran's synthesizer player Nick Rhodes
and his wife, model Julie-Anne, Paul King, Limahl,
EastEnders' soap star Anita Dobson and the eighties
answer to the Sex Pistols, Sigue, Sigue Sputnik.

Like all good Mercury bashes, this party, which cost
£50,000, carried on and on. It started at eleven o'clock
on a Saturday night and the last guest didn't leave till
five the next morning.

The body-painted beauties were created by a top
German artist, Bernd Bauer. It took five hours for

each girl to be painted and they were paid £100 each to display themselves to the guests. One of the models, Tracey Hicks, told me as the party reached its climax: 'I felt wonderful. It was just like I was a piece of art.' Mercury watched attentively as the girls paraded among the guests, his mouth breaking now and then into a huge smile. But he didn't believe in just watching at his parties: he believed in being the life and soul of them too, and one of the party's high spots was when the moustachioed star jumped on to a makeshift stage with former topless model turned singer Sam Fox to give an impromptu rock performance before his stunned guests. The couple ripped into a whole selection of rock classics including Little Richard's brilliantly nonsensical slab of three-minute sexual energy 'Tutti Frutti', during which Mercury held the big-busted model tight as he bumped and ground up against her. Afterwards he told me: 'We wanted everyone to have fun and I know that's exactly what they had.' He liked throwing parties because he believed they spread a little happiness.

Every one of Mercury's parties was an exotic extravaganza. For a thirty-ninth birthday bash, costing around £50,000, held in Munich he told the male guests to come in drag and then had the last laugh on them all by turning up in a bizarre concoction of gentlemanly attire, a Bavarian military jacket studded with medals and set off by harlequin trousers. Mercury filmed the event and planned to use footage of it for the video of his fourth solo single, 'Living On My Own'. A lot of top record company bosses and important showbusiness wheeler-dealers would have been severely embarrassed by this 'home movie' and in the end the idea was shelved. A highly placed record executive said the company had decided not to release the video because it could offend people.

Mercury himself said of the bash, attended by three hundred close friends: 'It was a great do. I had to have something lavish to face up to the thought of being forty! It was great that everyone entered into the spirit of the thing.'

At another extravaganza for the launch of the band's album *A Day At The Races*, a huge hospitality tent was hired at the Kempton racecourse and guests were treated to a magical afternoon's racing plus all the food and drink they could guzzle.

Sex was also an important element of Mercury's parties. At a New Orleans bash strippers performed such virtuoso acts as smoking cigarettes with their vaginas. That party, during which Mercury made a provocative entrance by sweeping in followed by twelve black-faced minstrels, also featured transsexual turns. Guests looked on in amazement as the beautiful full-breasted blondes they had been encouraging to climb out of their flimsy costumes turned out to be well-endowed men.

At another bash part of the cabaret involved a naked woman dancing with a live snake, while at the party I went to in Montreux the guests, assembled on a huge boat in the middle of a scenic Swiss lake, watched goggle-eyed as two strippers ripped off their clothes. For the launch of their album *Jazz*, Mercury and the band employed fifty nearly-naked girls to cycle around Wimbledon Stadium. It wasn't just gratuitous nudity: Brian May had written a song for the album called 'Fat Bottomed Girls', while Mercury was offering 'Bicycle Race'.

Freddie believed in arriving at his parties in style.

He had a helicopter whisk him from the band's show at Milton Keynes to London's elite Embassy nightclub, (whose owner Stephen Hayter also died of AIDS), though even that lightning mode of travel failed to get Mercury to the party in time to meet an idol of his, singer Diana Ross, who waltzed out just as the singer was waltzing in.

The best parties were held behind closed doors at Mercury's sumptuous Kensington home. Wayne Sleep, top ballet star and friend of Princess Diana, taught Mercury ballet after the Queen singer got in contact with him because he wanted to feature some ballet dancing in the band's video. Sleep, who has been to many of Mercury's bashes, told me: 'Freddie really knows how to throw a party. No expense is spared, he is so generous. He also loves to have themes. One party I went to at his home was a hat party. Everyone turned up in the strangest hats. I wrapped a curtain around my head and came as a turban.' At another party attended by Sleep the theme was shorts. It was held in Mercury's beautiful garden, which took up almost half an acre of prime Kensington land, and was a typically racy and riotous affair, even if reports that Sleep sent champagne glasses crashing and food flying when an airborne balletic manoeuvre he was attempting went badly wrong were inaccurate. According to Sleep, 'That never happened, but the party was wonderful. All his dos were.'

His birthday – Mercury was born on 5 September 1946 – was another great party day. Sometimes the parties could carry on for days on end. One such was the occasion of his thirty-fifth birthday, when he was in New York touring with the rest of the band. Determined to have his friends by his side to enjoy his birthday, he forked out thousands of pounds on first-class air tickets for them, then whisked them off to one of Manhattan's most exclusive hotels, where they proceeded to drink their way through £30,000 worth of the finest champagne. Recalling that event, which a former aide of Mercury's claimed cost £200,000, one of his closest friends, Peter Straker, said: 'He rented the entire suite of the Berkshire hotel on Central Park South which the management normally only let royalty have. But Freddie is a wonderfully generous person. He once spent thousands throwing a birthday party for me at his home. Nothing was ever too much trouble or money for him.'

Drugs, especially cocaine, were shared out freely at the parties – no doubt to help revellers make it through the nights. At one a dwarf passed among guests carrying bowls of the finest cocaine that money could buy. According to Peter Jones, one of Freddie's ex-minders, Mercury and a phalanx of party acolytes once blew £24,000 on cocaine in six weeks of wild living. At another bash Mercury, high on qualudes, smashed into the glass door of the restaurant he was partying in and then, when he attempted to go to the toilet, fell down a flight of stairs, bouncing on his head and oblivious to any pain. Jones was quoted as saying: 'Freddie took everything he could get his hands on – uppers, downers, pills and powders.'

Freddie's love of parties even gave him the opportunity to mix with royalty. At a bash after a charity gala featuring the Royal Ballet at Covent Garden he met Prince Andrew in the famous Crush Bar. The Prince was holding a plate of half-eaten strawberries and Mercury loudly summoned his assistant Peter Freestone to take it away. His voice rose above all the chatter in the crowded bar and he called out 'Phoebe', the lady's name he loved to call his valet. The Prince raised his eyebrows quizzically and remarked that he thought Freestone's name was Peter. Mercury then let the Prince into the secret of the pet name he had for his assistant.

At that meeting the Prince even gave the clothes obsessed showman some sartorial assistance when he fished the singer's long white scarf out of the drink in which it was dangling and wrung it out for him. But the Prince's request for the flamboyant front man to sing a song for him was met with an even more outrageous demand from Mercury, who told the Queen's handsome son that he would sing to him if Andrew would swing from the chandeliers first. Not surprisingly, this royal command performance did not take place. Nor did the Prince take up Mercury's invitation to accompany him to one of the capital's most outrageous gay nightclubs. Mercury told the Prince that he, some friends and a group of Royal Ballet dancers were going on to Heaven, the vast homosexual club just beside Charing Cross station. Prince Andrew was all set to go until his bodyguard put a damper on what would undoubtedly have been an evening to remember.

Mercury's last reported private party was in September 1987 for his forty-first birthday and it was as excellent and extravagant as all his others. He held it in Tony Pike's hotel on the island of Ibiza. Mercury hired a private DC 9 to whisk his close friends and showbusiness colleagues to a bash for five hundred special guests, which again cost the singer a little more than the price of an elegant apartment in Mayfair. It was one of his most theatrical. There was a lavish firework display which blazed Mercury's name across the Spanish sky, a cascade of swirling, sultry flamenco dancers and a twenty-foot birthday cake.

Mercury often claimed that his love of parties was instilled in him in those far-off Bombay days when he lived in the lap of luxury with servants carrying out his every whim. Whatever the truth of the matter, Mercury just loved to party and these parties were a perfect opportunity to meet the next Mr Right.

Pike's Hotel is a small, remote, five hundred year old former farmhouse tucked away on the island of Ibiza, and it was here that Freddie Mercury began to spend much of his holidays in the last seven years of his life.

In the eighties Ibiza was one of the most popular sunshine havens for the young with a reputation for easy sex, wild beach parties and carefree living. Like the young hedonists, Mercury wanted to taste the freedom of the idyllic Spanish island where he could escape from the world and simply be himself.

Mercury loved the privacy the hotel afforded him, the relaxed atmosphere, and the long sunshine-filled days sitting by the hotel's kidney-shaped pool. But it wasn't exactly love at first sight when Queen's manager Jim Beach introduced Freddie to the place, as the hotel's owner, an adventurous Australian, Tony Pike remembers.

'Freddie wanted to go somewhere quiet but he also wanted some fun.' It was a difficult combination, but Jim told Freddie that Pike's was the perfect place for him. Just as his chauffeur-driven car got to the bottom of the road, however Freddie, fed up that the journey seemed to be taking him to the middle of nowhere, stopped the car and demanded of Jim 'Where the bloody hell are you taking me?' Jim told him not to worry and get upset because he would love it the minute he saw it. Freddie pursed his lips, stared hard at Jim and said: 'Well I hope I do, because if I don't you're fired.'

And when Mercury was introduced to owner Tony Pike, in 1985 the first few minutes of the meeting did not augur well for the future. Mercury semed aloof and Pike believed he had a tetchy, demanding superstar on his hands. 'When I was introduced to him he just said hello and wasn't very friendly at all. I knew stars could be difficult and I thought this one was going to be exactly that. Things didn't improve when he went inside with his security people, gave one of the rooms the once over and declared "This ceiling is very low." I felt certain I was going to have a problem with him. I wanted to tell him that I had toiled for years building the place myself and everyone loved its quirkiness. I wanted to tell him that just because he was Freddie Mercury I didn't need any problems, when he suddenly waved his hand in the air and said: "Just joking." He started laughing, and I did too. And from that moment I realised he was going to be a great guy.'

From the first visit, Mercury began coming to Pike's regularly, often spending up to two weeks there at a time. 'Freddie did fall in love with the place,' said Pike, 'and often told me how great it was to be there. He said: "When I'm here, it's the first time I can stop being Freddie Mercury and just be myself."'

For the superstar who had previously lived his life at a breakneck pace Pike's provided a real opportunity to wind down.

'He really could relax here, and it was great to see him so happy. We spent an awful lot of time together. What endeared me to him was just how modest he was. A lot of the pop people play the big star all the time, but Freddie never did. I can still see his kind face when I'm talking to you, asking if he has been any trouble or if I really liked a record he made. He never took anything for granted and never revelled arrogantly in his superstardom.

'I remember the night he did his duet of "Barcelona" with Montserrat Caballé for a TV special. It was such a moving performance that some of the guys who were filming were actually crying. But when he came back to the hotel after the show, Freddie was just like a little boy, not a big superstar despite his sensational show. The audience had brought the house down, but Freddie still asked me in the bar that night: "Do you think they liked it?" And he wasn't seeking praise, he really wanted to be assured that his performance had been all right.

'Freddie was so human. He had so much warmth in him, and he wanted to be loved so much. That night we stayed talking till eight o'clock in the morning. He, a group of his close friends and me, just talked the night away. He was so excited about the show, his hands flying all over the place, and his voice getting higher and higher going "Oh, oh, oh!". It was magic.

'When you talked to Freddie, the conversation just flowed. There would not be any pauses, or embarrassing silences. When Freddie talked no one was ever at a loss as to what to say. He just drew you in as if by magic, and the time flew by.

'Freddie was a born raconteur. He told me the most amazing, funny stories, often camping it up something rotten. One of the most entertaining anecdotes he told was about when he was in Africa, travelling in the back of a landrover and a herd of elephants began chasing after him and knocking the landrover from side to side. The only thing in the back of the landrover was apples, so to defend himself Freddie started throwing them furiously at the angry herd to try to get them to stop in their tracks.

'The way he told it was so hilarious, and he was such a great story teller you could imagine him petrified in the back there trying to shake off the beasts with fruit. I can picture him right there even to this day because he told the story with so much life. Freddie was a wonderful story teller. He could never tell an anecdote just sitting in a chair. He had to get up and do all the actions. It was like watching a movie.'

When Freddie turned up to holiday at Pike's, he would hardly leave the property. Often the hotel's swimming pool would become the centre of Mercury's court: 'Sometimes everyone would get dressed up around the pool and really ham it down to the pool and Freddie would play for us. That was a wonderful experience. But despite the fact that Freddie loved to entertain, I think he was rather a shy person. He had a lot of humility in him which made him very endearing.

'He never liked to press himself on people. He never came across as "I'm a star" – in fact it was quite the opposite. Sometimes he would even apologise for himself. Often if his conversation got a little animated and there were other guests around he would say: "Please tell us if we are being too loud. I don't want to take over the place." He would often ask the other guests to join him so they wouldn't feel left out. He had incredibly good manners and was very polite.'

'Sometimes when he invited other guests to join them, a couple would think he was either showing off or being condescending and would say that they didn't need him to buy them a drink. I would have to take them aside, and explain that he really didn't mean it like that and he just wanted them to spend some time with him. They would join him and get to know him and the next day apologise to me for taking him the wrong way. Everybody always ended up saying what a hell of a guy he was.

'Freddie was a very, very warm human being. When people make the kind of money he made or are as famous as he was, they are usually not too concerned about the small, everyday things. But Freddie was very different. He would remember a person's name, their birthday, something they had done together a year ago. It was quite remarkable and made him very endearing.

'A number of people have said he was a lonely guy, but I never found that. If he chose to be alone it was because he chose to be and that was all there was to it. All the people who knew him, including me and other people he met casually, loved him. He only had to call and people would be there. He invited me to a couple of his parties and I never had any hesitation about accepting because I always knew that wherever Freddie was, there was fun.'

It was in the genial surroundings of Pike's that Mercury managed to overcome his phobia of water. 'Freddie was very frightened of water,' said Pike, 'and hated going on it, but one day I managed to talk him into coming out with me on my boat. As he got used to it, he gradually relaxed and after that he would come out regularly with me. We would sit out on the boat, basking in the sunshine, drinking Pimms Number One or champagne to cool us down and listening to wonderful music. Other times I would take him to another nearby island called Formenterra.'

The boat journey which cured Mercury was to the Isomele de Sel, a former salt mill, which had been turned into an elevated restaurant with magnificent sea views. 'When I suggested to him that he should go on the boat he said: "You'll never get me on your boat my dear". And then I said: "Listen you'll love the restaurant", and he thought about it for a minute and then suddenly said: "Will you promise to look after me?" I told him I would, and the deal was done. He was a little nervous at first but then he loved it.'

'When his friends found out what he had done they were stunned. Phoebe [Peter Freestone], who had been his Man Friday for years, just couldn't believe that Freddie had beaten his fear of water. But then the Freddie I knew loved living life to the full. He was a pretty wild sort of guy. He worked very hard – harder than ten men – but he played hard too and that is a rare combination, and about the most perfect mix you can have.

'He appealed to everyone – even people who were homophobic. Lots of people told me they hated gays but when they saw Freddie that hatred went. He was just an absorbing character who really charmed people, but not in a false way. He had so much personality. He was so thoughtful. Over even the slightest things. For instance he would be in the restaurant sitting down at a table for twenty when suddenly he would notice that someone was missing a wine glass. He would immediately insist that they took his and would wait patiently till another wine glass was brought to him.

'Freddie liked a nice wine – red wine, white wine, he was always very appreciative of anything we served. I haven't got the best chefs in the world and sometimes dishes weren't that good, but I never heard Freddie complain or anything. He always said, "That's marvellous my dear."'

Pike's was where Mercury held one of his most exotic parties. 'Freddie was going to have a party with Elton John,' recalls Pike, 'but things went wrong when Elton's manager and Jim Beach had a row in the bar and the whole thing had to be called off. Freddie was distraught and absolutely furious. A short while afterwards he came up to me and told me: "Look, it's my birthday in four days' time, and birthdays are a time of celebration. I want the best bloody party this island has ever seen." He got it too. There were about seven hundred guests, forty-seven entertainers and a spectacular firework display that could be seen all over the island. That night I opened three hundred and fifty bottles of the finest French champagne and they were all drained completely dry.'

But it was a party where nobody ate cake. 'Freddie had a cake made in the shape of the Gaudí cathedral in Barcelona which was one of his favourite buildings, and I flew it over to the party in a private plane. Unfortunately when the plane came in it did a bad landing and the whole cake collapsed. When Freddie heard the news he was mortified and said to me: "You've got to do something. We can't have a party without a cake." There was only about four hours to go before the guests arrived so between us we had a brainwave. We made a cake that was two metres

Frederick Balsara, in his art student days at the
Ealing School of Art. (*Photo:* Daily Mail)

By April 1974 Mercury's photographs were more poised and more sophisticated - Queen was in the charts and in the news. *Clockwise from top left:* John Deacon, Roger Taylor, Freddie Mercury, Brian May. (*Photo:* S. I.)

Freddie Mercury and Brian May in the No.1 chartbusting 'Bohemian Rhapsody'. (*Photo:* S. I.)

The kings of rock in 1976. *From left:* Brian May, Roger Taylor, Freddie Mercury, John Deacon. (*Photo:* S. I.)

Mercury's style was unique off stage — and on.
(*Photo:* S. I.)

Freddie Mercury — Superman. (*Photo:* S. I.)

Queen's hit single 'Radio Ga Ga' reached No.2 in the British charts. (*Photo:* S. I.)

Live Aid, the global rock show that rocked the world, raised nearly £50 million and made Freddie and Queen even more mega-stars. (*Photo:* S. I.)

Crowning glory — the king of Queen in command of his audience. (*Photo:* S. I.)

On stage in front of a swaying mass of fans,
Newcastle 1986. (*Photo:* S. I.)

An epic performance at Victoria Docks in London's
East End. (*Photo:* Daily Mail)

Freddie practises an unorthodox backhand in Ibiza.
(*Photo:* Eugene Adebari)

Bachelors of the arts. *From left:* Roger Taylor (who graduated in biology), Brian May (physics), Freddie Mercury (graphic design) and John Deacon (electrical engineering). (*Photo:* Famous)

Freddie talks to the author — on the record.
(*Photo:* Famous)

After a classic triumph: Freddie and his heroine
Montserrat Caballe. (*Photo:* Famous)

Peter Straker and Madame Jo Jo with the ever-recognisable Freddie. (*Photo:* Famous)

Freddie with Mary Austin, the girl from Biba who became his close friend. (*Photo:* Famous)

For once Freddie isn't holding the mike — but Sam Fox is... (*Photo:* Famous)

Page Three girl and rock mega-star sing an unlikely duet. (*Photo:* Famous)

Two of the most adored stars of pop: Freddie with the ever-youthful Cliff Richard. (*Photo:* Famous)

The ultimate showman — two classic Mercury poses.
(*Photos:* Daily Mail)

long, decorated with all the notes from Freddie and Montserrat's duet "Barcelona". Freddie was thrilled.'

But despite all their efforts the cake was never 'consummated'. Adds Pike: 'It was a tragedy. The cake looked fantastic and six men carried it out. But when we put in on the table no one wanted to eat it. I guess there were too many other things to do. In the end four of the guests grabbed hold of my secretary, Penny, and threw her right into the cake despite her screams. That's what Freddie's parties were like . . .'

That was also the party when the whole hotel almost went up in smoke. Recalls Pike: 'We had hundreds of ballons all blown up in black and gold around the courtyard and someone went to pop one of them with a cigarette. A whole wall went up in a massive sheet of flames. It looked incredible, because the flames went up about 100 feet in the air. But it could have been a disaster.'

When the reports of Mercury's illness began to filter from Britain Pike tried to find out what was wrong. 'I asked some of the people closest to him because I was very worried when I heard it was AIDS. But they all said that he hadn't got that but a blood disease he had caught on tour in Brazil. Now, of course, I realise that everyone was trying to protect him.'

Tony Pike was on a boat off the North island of New Zealand when he heard the news that Mercury was dead: 'I couldn't believe it. I just went numb. It was dreadful news. The guy was a bloody genius. His death was a tragedy for everybody who knew him.

'Freddie was extremely emotional which makes a person very vulnerable and that's why some people never got that close to him. He had to trust you, believe in you and have a feeling for you before he would let you into his world but once you were there it was magical. Freddie, unlike many stars, had true friends around him and he was always very loyal to those people. And when you got to know him you found out just how much fun he could be. And in a way that was why he was such an enigma because he was so serious and so clever in his work but when he played he played better than anyone I know.

'I have nothing but great memories of him. As I'm talking to you, I can still see that warm friendly face and hear that infectious laugh. For me he will never die.'

Apart from music Freddie Mercury was torn between two passions — sex and spending money. To the flamboyant singer both were orgasmic events which left him in a state of rapture.

In a few minutes of ecstatic shopping Mercury was capable of spending more money than most people earn in a lifetime. When I asked him once how he coped with his wealth and whether he ever felt guilty at the millions he made, Mercury was bemused by the question. Throwing his hands dramatically in the air, he declared: 'I've always coped extremely well with wealth. I don't believe in hoarding my money away in a bank.

'I love to spend, spend, spend. After all, that's what money is there for. I'm not like some of these stars who are obsessed with counting their pennies.'

His love of spending money was something that predated his success in the pop world. When one of Britain's top publicists, Tony Brainsby, decided to represent the band it was one of the first things that struck him about Mercury. Brainsby, who has represented a host of top acts including Paul McCartney Stevie Wonder and Jayne Mansfield told me: 'When I first started working with them, Freddie still had a stall in Kensington Market and not very much money to his name. But even then he loved spending money as if it was going out of fashion. He believed money was for buying things.'

Mercury's spending sprees were legendary. Once he made a lightning trip to Japan and came back with £250,000 worth of antiques and art. Another time he spent a similar amount on an exquisite 144-piece dinner service handpainted with miniature copies of Constable paintings and edged with gold filigree, each serving dish costing £20,000. During one of his many trips to Harrods he bought up an entire exhibition of Chinese furniture, and he was always searching for Dresden dolls to add to his valuable collection. He even spent £50,000 on fish, filling the forty-five-foot pond in his garden with brightly coloured koi carp, a Japanese fish which can live up to a hundred years, some specimens of which can cost thousands of pounds each.

Exclusive London jewellers Cartier would stay open for Mercury after hours so that he could shop peacefully for gems and gold. And tours weren't just for staging concerts for his devoted fans all around the world, they were also a chance to buy more goodies from the furthest corners of the earth. Mercury, followed by a train of porters bearing freshly acquired antiques and artefacts, was a familiar sight at many of the world's most exclusive hotels.

Fine art was his passion and he amassed one of the best collections in Britain. It took in Japanese woodcuts, Impressionist paintings and works by Victorian masters and Russian fantasy painter Marc Chagall and was worth millions. Trips to auction rooms and art galleries were a regular occurence in Mercury's life and continued even when AIDS was doing its upmost to strike him down. According to Roxy Meade, the singer's publicist when he died, 'Freddie would go through collecting phases. There were so many things he loved. And he had exquisite taste. It was never tacky like so many showbusiness stars.'

Mercury himself once told me: 'Some days when I am feeling down, I just love to go out on huge shopping sprees and lose myself in my money. It is a bit like a woman buying herself a new hat to cheer herself up. Though sometimes at the end of one of these binges I do think: 'Oh dear, what on earth have I bought now?'

He spent money like it was going out of circulation and when tax advisors urged the star to keep on spending it was as much of a turn-on as whispered words of passion in the night. But he rarely carried money – 'like the real Queen' he once quipped – and employees and close friends were often put in charge of his cash and credit cards as they followed him on his shopping blow-outs. 'All my money goes to Sotheby's, Christie's, Harrods, Asprey and Cartier,' he said. 'I believe in being extravagant. Sometimes all I really want from life is to make pots of money and then go off and spend it.'

Mercury's biggest extravagance was his gorgeous house in Kensington, which he bought for £500,000 in hard cash. Mary Austin found the huge Edwardian house for the singer while he was on tour and sent him pictures of it. Mercury was instantly smitten. He rang her immediately, as excited as a kid at Christmas, told her he had to have it and to go ahead with the purchase. Film director Mike Hodges, who made *Flash Gordon*, for which he drafted Queen in to do the soundtrack, remembered: 'Freddie was absolutely thrilled when he bought the house. He would come in with pictures of it and show them to everyone.'

Mercury was as perfectionist about the house (originally built for the merchant banking family Hoare) in fashionable Kensington as he was about his work. He hired a team of architects and decorators to work to his exact specifications and it was four years before he actually moved in. It took so long to get ready, with Mercury continually changing and adding to his original plans, that the singer would often joke to friends that he was unlikely ever to move in. And he told me during one of our interviews: 'I have had this house for four years now. It is quite exquisite and gorgeous . . . Our people are still working on it, putting up all kinds of elaborate s***. At this rate I will probably move in when I am old and grey.'

When the house was finally finished it boasted eight bedrooms, four marble bathrooms, a jacuzzi and a minstrel's gallery. The *pièce de résistance* was Mercury's ornate bedroom on the top floor, which was created by knocking three of the original rooms together and included a balcony with Romanesque columns together with an emperor-sized bed fitted with an electronic console controlling a variety of gadgets.

Above the bed, which had to be hoisted up to the top floor by crane, was an enormous domed roof concealing hundreds of multicoloured lights designed to change the room's atmosphere to suit Mercury's every mood and whim. The sophisticated, gadget-packed system cost tens of thousand of pounds and could create the effect of sunrise, daytime, sunset and night-time at the touch of a switch.

The bedroom, like many of the other rooms, housed various antique treasures and *objets d'art*. Covering the floor was a handmade pure wool carpet with a star motif in the middle which would flicker and glow as light was shone on it. Next door was a huge mahogany dressing room, lined with mirrors and housing the singer's extensive collection of clothes which he had begun as a stallholder in Kensington Market. The bathrooms too were palatial. One of the main ones was done out entirely in black marble, the other in orange marble, and both were fitted with a sea of mirrors.

According to Phil Symes, another of Mercury's publicists, 'Freddie did everything so tastefully. He had some wonderful furniture and antiques but, though he had a lot of possessions, the house was never cluttered. Everything was very well co-ordinated.

'One of the most beautiful rooms was the living room with its polished wood floor and beautiful galleried area.'

In one of his more dramatic moments Mercury confessed: 'I have everything that money can buy except happiness.' But like many of the things he said, it was a white lie that sounded much better than the truth. In those halcyon days of never-ending shopping and sex, Mercury was thrilled by every new acquisition. A more accurate comment was his confession 'I'm fortunate enough to be rich. Sometimes I believe the only bit of happiness I can create is with my money.'

Although the singer loved to indulge himself and his whims, he also loved to extend his largesse to acquaintances, friends and, of course, lovers. He was one of the most generous stars in the rock world and would reward those close to him not only with 'baubles and trinkets' but also with plush cars and homes. Often he would head for Harrods, as his shopping spree fever raged, spend thousands of pounds on presents. It was once reported that he spent £5,000 on perfume for every woman he knew. 'My spending furies are never wasted,' he said. 'I have so many friends I can give things to. I love splashing out on other people. It's worth it just to see the smile on their faces.' One gift he could never buy, however, was a new home for his parents, who, despite all Mercury's offers, refused to move from their small semi-detached house in Feltham under Heathrow's noisy flight path.

Even just months away from the end he was spending money on himself, buying up more valuable paintings, and on his close circle of friends. In the year of his death he went house-hunting, spending around £1 million on homes for ten of his closest friends. And sources close to the star believe he spent much more of his estimated fortune of £28 million on friends during those last few months. When he was bedridden, friends say he would look through fine art catalogues, still dreaming of more luxuries to spend his fortune on.

Mercury once joked that when he died he would like to be buried with all his treasures like the Pharoahs of ancient Egypt. It was a wish that could never come true: there wasn't an underground vault big enough.

Chapter 7

LIVE AID

The Concert That Rocked the World

*'We're still as poncy as ever
but we are capable of doing things'*

It was the rock concert that was billed as the greatest show on earth – and for once the pop hype was justified. The Live Aid show boasted what was a who's who of the world's biggest pop talent, including Paul McCartney, Elton John, David Bowie, U2, Dire Straits, the Who, Phil Collins, Eric Clapton, Madonna, Mick Jagger and Sting. Altogether the two shows – one in London's Wembley Stadium, the other in Philadelphia's JFK Stadium – were watched by two billion people in a hundred and seventy countries around the world, the biggest ever TV audience for any rock event.

The show had been put together by a former punk rocker, the opinionated leader of the Boomtown Rats, Bob Geldof, and its purpose was to raise money for the tragic famine that was decimating Ethiopia. Geldof, dubbed Saint Bob for his work, decided on the idea of a charity rock show, bigger than any the world had ever seen, after watching a report about Ethiopia on British television. Through constant harassment, chicanery and friendly persuasion he managed to put on an event that exceeded anyone's wildest dreams.

Both concerts on that hot day of 13 July 1985 were runaway successes, with act after act doing their bit for charity as the world looked on. In London the show kicked off in the presence of Prince Charles and Princess Diana at midday with headbanger Status Quo urging fans to start 'Rockin' All Over The World'. That is exactly what the huge global audience and the bands did for the next sixteen hours, when the concert in Philadelphia finally came to a close.

There were some magnificent performances that day, the enormity of the event bringing out the very best from the performers. But at Wembley one group stole the show from all the others – Queen. They came on just before seven on that warm Saturday evening and as British comedians Griff Rhys Jones and Mel Smith introduced them, the crowd of seventy thousand erupted. Mercury strutted on stage, sporting white singlet vest, powder-blue jeans and silver amulet, as the band launched into their tough rocking 'Hammer To Fall'. Mercury dominated the stage like a colossus, throwing poses left, right and centre, riveting the audience with his every move and gesture. Within minutes the singer had the crowd eating out of the palm of his hand as he rushed up and down, backwards, forwards, every which way, his cut-off microphone dancing with each movement like a frenzied limb. He and the band belted out some of their biggest hits, including 'Bohemian Rhapsody' and 'Radio GaGa', as the crowd went wild. At every cheer Mercury drove his band on and on, pushing them to the limit, his own face wildly contorted and streaming with sweat.

Later he was to say: 'I have to win people over. If I don't, I don't consider the performance a success. You have to give it everything, until you know you've got every person with you. Every time I step out on stage I want to make sure that people have a great time.'

That day Mercury and Queen gave an incredible performance and transformed themselves into superstars, leaving two billion people in awe of their power and magnetism. Pop superstar Elton John, himself, admitted that the band stole the show from every other act. They had just twenty minutes to give the performance of their lives and it was twenty minutes that pop fans wished could have gone on for ever. Their set was pure rock theatre, displaying Mercury's electrical stage presence and his powerful vocal talents to their fullest. After, kicking off with 'Hammer To Fall', they proceeded to whip the crowd into a frenzy with some of their best-known classics, including 'Crazy Little Thing Called Love', 'Bohemian Rhapsody', which had the huge crowd singing along, and, most apt of all, 'We Are The Champions'. The crowd chanted and clapped to every beat of the hypnotic 'Radio GaGa', while during 'We Are The Champions' an awesome sea of seventy thousand bodies swayed in unison.

Mercury said afterwards: 'We wanted to perform all the songs that people were familiar with and could identify with. The concert may have come out of a terrible human tragedy, but we wanted to make it a joyous occasion.' And that day he proved himself master of everything. He took to the keyboards for 'Rhapsody', the guitar for 'Crazy Little Thing . . .' and even found time to fool around with one of the BBC's cameramen.

Just before the star-studded finale, when all the bands came on stage for a rousing version of the Live Aid anthem, 'Do They Know It's Christmas?', the biggest-selling British single of all time, Queen were back to give the crowd more. Mercury and May sang the appropriate and moving 'Is This The World We Created?', from the album *The Works*, and were greeted with rapturous applause. 'It's very odd,' said Freddie, 'but we composed that particular song well before the Live Aid project. It was a song we wrote about the suffering and starvation of children all over the planet and it matched the situation so well that we decided that was definitely one song we would do.'

The tabloid headlines echoed the crowd's reaction, screaming: 'Queen are King!' and informing the few people who hadn't seen the show how Mercury and his band had totally dominated the day. London's *Daily Mirror* called their performance 'simply superb', and the show's organiser Bob Geldof confirmed: 'Queen were absolutely the best band of the day, whatever your personal preference.'

Brian May said later: 'The rest of us played OK, but Freddie was out there and took it to a new level altogether. It wasn't just Queen fans – he connected with everyone.' What many of the fans both at Wembley and around the world did not know was that apparently Mercury had been advised by doctors not to sing at the star-studded show because of a throat infection, but had decided to carry on regardless, determined not to disappoint his fans.

Queen's Live Aid triumph proved more than enough to make up for the disappointment of not being involved in the Band Aid single 'Do They Know It's Christmas?' The group were out of the country on their European tour while the single was being recorded. 'We felt very left out,' said Freddie a few days before the show, 'but we're so glad we are a part of it this time.' The Ethiopian disaster had been playing on Mercury's mind for some time and he was glad he, along with others in the pop world, could do something about it: 'When I first saw the television report it disturbed me so deeply that I just couldn't bear to watch it. I had to switch the television off.' But he denied that the band cancelled all other engagements in order to take part out of a sense of guilt: 'I have never felt guilty about being rich and those feelings weren't there when I decided to perform in Live Aid. What I felt was sheer sorrow and a deep upset that something like this was going on in our world and I felt for a time quite, quite helpless. The point of this concert is to wake people up to the starvation and famine, to make everyone realise just what is going on and to do something positive that will hopefully touch people and make them dig into their pockets.'

But it was a show that it was particularly important for Queen to do. In August of the previous year they had upset the liberal world of rock and roll by performing at the South African venue Sun City, where they played seven sell-out shows. The band found themselves promptly put on the United Nations cultural blacklist, suspended by the Musicians' Union and fined. They appealed and eventually the decision to blacklist them was reversed. Still it was a 'mistake' that alienated the band from much of the rock world and gave them a lot of bad publicity, so when the chance to appear on Live Aid was offered, the group saw an opportunity to make amends. They were determined to put on the show of their lives and disappeared into a studio for two whole days to rehearse their twenty-minute set, over and over again. This time they wanted to make sure nothing went wrong. 'We spent more time getting ready for this and rehearsing than we did for some of our world tours,' said Brian May. 'We wanted to give the best twenty minutes we possibly could.'

It proved a vital turning point in the band's popularity. Queen had been relatively quiet in 1982 and had taken all of 1983 off as a sabbatical. They had re-emerged on the scene in 1984 with the album *The Works*, which spawned a series of hits, including 'I Want To Break Free' (which reached number five), 'It's A Hard Life' (number six) and 'Hammer To Fall' (number thirteen). Their biggest hit of the year was the delightful 'Radio GaGa', which would have hit the number one spot if it hadn't been kept off the top by Frankie Goes To Hollywood's million-selling 'Relax'. The Live Aid show brought Queen to the new generation. Suddenly Freddie Mercury had won millions of new fans and wasn't an 'old fart' responsible for some dramatically camp songs in the seventies. It was Live Aid which saw the band make the step from playing arenas to stadiums. In 1984 they were playing four nights at Wembley Arena, which holds nine thousand; in 1986, the year after the Live Aid Show, they sold out Wembley Stadium for two nights (150,000) and Knebworth (120,000). Added to that were the crowds of eighty thousand plus on most nights of the European tour for that same year.

All the band were of course aware of this uneasy mix of charity and commerciality and recognized that the Live Aid platform would give them tremendous exposure all over the world. The night before the show drummer Roger Taylor said: 'Of course, it is a wonderful cause and will make a pot of money for that wonderful cause, but make no mistake – we're doing it for our own glory as well.' The week after Live Aid, the band's *Greatest Hits* album shot back up the charts, leaping a massive fifty places, and *The Works* became a hit all over again. Queen's sales were estimated to have increased fivefold as the world woke up to their music. Mercury's debut solo album *Mr Bad Guy* rocketed back into the charts, climbing forty places, and tripling its sales after the show.

Yet the sales, though welcome, were really insignificant beside the occasion itself and what it was about. Live Aid had tapped a vein of warmth, generosity and caring that had rarely manifested itself in the pop world before. Queen themselves were so impressed by the Live Aid show that they recorded a single dedicated to the man behind it all, Bob Geldof. 'One Vision' was a tribute to Geldof's determination to help the suffering in Africa and proved a massive smash in November 1985, reaching number seven. 'Bob Geldof has done a remarkable thing,' said Freddie at the time of Live Aid. 'It took someone like him to have the drive and determination to get something like this together and make it work so successfully. I have the highest respect and admiration for him.'

Chapter 8

SOMEBODY TO LOVE

The Men and Women
in Freddie Mercury's Life

'Love is Russian roulette for me'

As a star right up there in the pop stratosphere, Freddie Mercury could indulge in a hectic and adventurous sex life, often having a different lover every night. There were plenty of people ready to go to bed with the singer, who once confessed to 'an enormous sex drive'. But Mercury also had a romantic side, a side that loved the idea of having a special person in his life, someone who could share in the magical world he created around him, could give him the love he so desperately needed, and who could comfort and care for him during the bad times.

Mercury would vacillate between these two extremes throughout the period of his superstardom until he discovered that he had contracted AIDS. But if the singer loved the idea of spending his life with one special person, the reality was very different. As a rock star he was spoilt for sex – for when it comes to aphrodisiacs fame is much more powerful than oysters, rhino horns or alligator tails. 'I'll go to bed with anything,' he once admitted. 'And my bed is so huge it can comfortably sleep six. I prefer my sex without any involvement. There are times when I just lived for sex.' And during one interview he told me: 'I am a very sexual person. I f*** all the time, though I am much more choosy now than I used to be.'

According to his friends Mercury went to bed with hundreds of men. Many who knew him said he had a great fear of spending time alone – especially at night – and, in his more dramatic outpourings, Mercury himself once confessed that when he was alone he would often wake up in the middle of the night in a cold sweat. His huge sexual appetite was the talking point of a birthday party he once threw in London, where many of the guests gave him sex aid toys as presents. And it was no coincidence he chose to spend much of his time in Munich and New York, two hotbeds of the homosexual scene, with their numerous gay bars and discos. On tour he revelled in sex. After a scintillating show, he would do a night of hectic clubbing, and in these clubs there was always a procession of men eager to meet him.

Mercury often said that his promiscuity was an attempt to cure the loneliness he felt, or to heal over the scars left by a number of his relationships. While there may have been a grain of truth in this, he felt he had to defend what to many might seem unpalatable – his liking for straightforward sex without any kind of emotional involvement. Mercury enjoyed sex for sex's sake and there was no real need for him to explain it away. But he also liked the comfort and security that a steady relationship brings and tried to juggle these conflicting needs: 'I want to have my cake and eat it too,' he admitted. 'I want my security but I also want my freedom.'

When Mercury talked about love the arrogant star he became on stage could turn ultra-soft: 'I'm very vulnerable, but only when I really let people get near me. I build up a big defence. It happens automatically. I can be very over-emotional and that can be a very destructive trait in me.

'I am a romantic, but I do put up a barrier around myself, so it is hard for people to get in and to know the real me. I fall in love much too quickly and that results in me getting badly hurt. Maybe I just draw the wrong kind of people to me. The problem with love is that you lose control and that is a very vulnerable state to be in. I would love to really have a beautiful relationship with somebody, but it never seems to work out. What I would like most of all is to be in a state of blissful love.'

And in one particularly vulnerable interview, when I asked him if there was anything that the man who seemed to have everything still wanted, he admitted: 'Happiness. I haven't got that. Yes, I have thousands of friends, but you can seem to have everything, and yet have nothing. Maybe one day I'll catch up with myself and that will be my downfall.'

After he finished his relationship with his only long-time girlfriend, Mary Austin, Mercury explored his homosexuality to the fullest, often having a different male lover every night. The Queen front man told his closest friends that he first had a homosexual relationship at boarding school in India at the age of fourteen. But if Mercury was promiscuous during his wilder days, he always liked to have a regular boyfriend, to share whatever part of the world he had chosen as his base, and the conflict between his promiscuity and his need for a steady relationship propelled him into some furious rows with his lovers. The band's lengthy tours, when they were away from home for months on end, were often Mercury's most frenetic bed-hopping periods. While the other members of the band and the group's roadies might go off to a strip club or a disco, Mercury would head off for the town's gay area to see what the night had to offer. He found New York a particularly thrilling place: 'When I am there, I just slut myself. It is Sin City with a capital S.'

Barbara Valentin, the busty German film actress who became one of Mercury's closest friends when the singer lived in Munich, revealed how men at gay clubs would make a beeline for him whenever he came in. And a guest at one of the parties Mercury held on Ibiza remembers how 'a lot of the local rough trade were rounded up on the island and herded up to the party' to make sure it went with a bang. But Mercury's romps often had a sense of high camp and fun about them. One hotel guest on Ibiza recalls how Mercury and a handsome young man he had been lounging with by the hotel's pool leapt around trying to smack each other's bottoms and screaming: 'Take that, you bitch!'

In the early eighties Mercury exchanged his long hair and feminine stage wear for a new strong image. He cut his hair short, grew a moustache and strutted around in leathers. It was a uniform that gay men had adopted and Mercury's new look also indicated the kind of men he was himself attracted to – one friend said that his dream date would be someone who looked like American beefcake actor Burt Reynolds, who, unfortunately for Mercury, happened to be totally heterosexual. He was proud of his 'build' too. When he caught someone staring at the bulge in his trousers, he told them: 'That's all my own work. There's not a coke bottle stuffed down there or anything.'

But in all the interviews he did Mercury never really admitted to his gayness. He referred vaguely to having tried relationships with 'both men and women', but that was as far as his revelations went. Usually he would say something like 'If people want to know whether I'm gay, I never tell them. Instead I say they should try to find out for themselves. People can think what they like about my bi-sexual image. And that's what I want them to do. I want to keep my mystique around me.'

Most of the band's fans either never realised the extent of Mercury's homosexuality or refused to believe the rumours. To many of his female fans he was an ideal potential husband. One declared: 'He is my Mr Perfect. He isn't seen in public with girls because he has one special lady in his life whom he lives with and who he wants to protect from the glare of the spotlight. But if he were to ever give her up, I'd be only too happy to step into her shoes. Freddie just has so much charisma and compassion.'

Just why Mercury never admitted he was gay to the world at large and repeatedly trivialised, joked or skirted round the issue is a secret the singer took with him to his grave. Some friends believe he didn't want to upset his strictly religious parents, others feel that as an intensely private man he never really gave out many details about himself – this is borne out by the few interviews he did and the way he hardly ever discussed his background. Others still feel that, as an astute businessman, he felt parading and pontificating about his gayness could lose him many fans. In America this was borne out when people started throwing razor blades at the singer in concerts when he changed his image, affected butch clothes and grew a moustache which many fans rightly interpreted as a gay signal.

The backlash increased when the *I Want To Break Free* video, featuring all the band in drag, was shown in America. Though Britain saw it as a tongue-in-cheek bit of fun, the Americans did not see the joke. Brian May said at the time: 'Everyone in Britain thought the video was just a laugh but in America they hated it and thought it was an insult'.

But a gay colleague of Mercury's denied the star had a problem with his sexuality. He said: I spent a lot of time with Freddie and I never felt being gay actually mattered to him. I think he was totally at ease with it all. I admired him for that because he was never bothered by it the way some people are, he wasn't ashamed about it at all. That was Freddie's beauty. He thought, 'I like men, so what?' He never made a big deal of it.

'Of course lots of men were always hitting on him because of who he was, but it was never a problem. He handled it all so well because he was so at ease with it. Then of course he thought how lucky he was to be able to have such a great sex life.'

Paul Prenter, Mercury's former personal manager, worked with the singer for nine years and witnessed his wild homosexual flings at first hand. He, too, was eventually to die of AIDS, three months before Mercury. He infuriated the singer when he sold the story of his times with Mercury to the British tabloid

The Sun. He told the paper about Mercury's sexual conquests and how he loved to cruise gay bars and clubs, finally getting to bed at seven the next morning and rarely alone. To keep himself going, Prenter says, Mercury would shovel cocaine up his nose, always sharing it with those around him, and often blowing £500 weekly on the fashionable drug to get him through the night.

Prenter claimed that in all the time he was with the singer Mercury never slept with a woman again. He also revealed how two of Mercury's former lovers, Tony Bastin, whom he met at a gay club in Brighton, and John Murphy, an airline steward whom the singer met on a flight to New York, had both died of AIDS. After their deaths Mercury became petrified that he would die of AIDS himself and poured out his fears to Prenter.

After Mercury left Munich suddenly in 1985, Valentin said he became a changed man, preferring to stay at his Kensington home instead of raving it up at clubs and filling his life with new men. Many of Mercury's other friends noticed this sudden change and were puzzled by it – it was as if he had suddenly become another person. But the singer explained it away, saying: 'I am a person of extremes. I can shift from black to white quite easily. I don't like anything in between. Grey has never been a favourite colour of mine.'

And so he shut the door on his hectic, globe-trotting days and his nights of sexual adventure and exploration. After his spells in Munich, New York and Switzerland, Mercury decided to make London his home. He set up house in his Kensington mansion and gradually began to retreat from the rest of the world. It was there that he was to live sedately with a former hairdresser, Jim Hutton, who was Mercury's last regular boyfriend, and who stayed with the singer till the bitter end.

There weren't many women who flowered in the hothouse that was Freddie Mercury's life – but a former boutique manageress, Mary Austin, was an exception to the boys-only rule.

Delicate, blonde Mary Austin was, in fact, his closest friend. The couple first met in the early seventies and their devoted friendship to each other was to continue right up to Mercury's tragic death. Their paths first crossed in the Biba boutique in Kensington Church Street, just a few platform-booted strides from the stall that Mercury used to work in.

Biba was the boutique of the late sixties and early seventies, and it wasn't just a clothes shop, more a way of life. The young flocked to the incense-perfumed, fern-decorated emporium to buy what the store's owner, Barbara Hulanicki, told them was 'in'. It had beautiful clothes, seemingly old-fashioned, yet quite up to the minute, all dyed in the most exotic colours, and though it was primarily a women's boutique men flocked there too and bought its T-shirts, underwear and jumpers in the androgynous fashion of the times. Mercury was one of the men who shopped at Biba's and Mary Austin one of the impossibly beautiful girls, decked out in maroon lipstick and matching tights, who worked in its languidly chic atmosphere.

Later on the shop moved to the old Derry and Toms building in Kensington High Street, on the top floor of which, transformed into the Roof Gardens Club, Mercury was later to have one of his parties. When Biba took over Derry and Toms it boasted of being the biggest boutique in the world with five floors and two hundred thousand square feet of clothes, selling style with a capital S and attracting gawping tourists from all over the world. But the Church Street shop possessed an intimacy and sensuality that the huge store in Kensington High Street never had. What's more, it was a perfect pick-up place.

Mercury told me: 'I met Mary around 1970 and ever since then we have had a wonderful relationship. I met her at the Biba boutique, where she worked. I was a Biba freak right from the beginning, way before it got turned into a big department store. When I used to go there it was just a small boutique.

'Mary and I were closer than anybody else, though we stopped living together after about seven years. But I still see her every day and I am as fond of her now as I have ever been. She only lives about two minutes from me now.'

When Mercury was dying Mary was one of the people most affected, emerging from his Kensington home close to tears almost every day after keeping a vigil by his bed. And it was Mary who broke the news of Mercury's death to the singer's distraught parents.

Mercury and the frail blue-eyed beauty were originally lovers and lived in a cluttered Holland Park flat a few minutes' walk from where they both worked. As Mercury began to come to terms with his gayness, his relationship with Mary became platonic in nature. But even when the singer embarked on a procession of gay affairs – some casual, some long-lasting – he and Mary were still as devoted, if not more devoted, to each other. Explaining what to many people seemed a bizarre and hopeless relationship, he told me: 'Mary and I have a good understanding. She gives me the freedom that I need. I am not built to be a family man. I am much too restless and highly strung for that.

'Mary is very independent about the life I lead. But it is a kind of understanding that doesn't come overnight. She has learned not to get jealous over me. We have gone through a lot of ups and downs in our times together, but that has made our relationship all the stronger. I know a lot of people find it difficult to understand our relationship and, yes, it is an odd bond, but other people who come into our lives just have to accept it. We love each other very much and look after each other.'

Mary herself once said that if Mercury had been heterosexual there would have been no doubt that they would have married. According to Mercury, the couple had discussed the possibility of marrying, and at various times in his life, though often in his more melodramatic moods, he declared that Mary was his only close friend and that when he died he would leave the bulk of his fortune, estimated at around £28 million, to her. It wasn't just an idle boast: Mercury looked after Mary, financially, as well as any husband looks after a wife. When they stopped living together he bought her a spectacular four-bedroomed flat just minutes away from his new home, so that they could see each other every day. And when Mercury died, of all his friends it was Mary who made the most emotional tribute to him. In a voice as frail as a sigh she murmured: 'I feel a great sense of loss and pain and I am sure there are lots of fans who share that loss. I never ever stopped loving Freddie and I don't think he ever stopped loving me.'

As Mercury embarked on his string of gay affairs, Mary decided to find romance elsewhere. She had a four-year relationship with musician Jo Burt, a former member of Tom Robinson's band Sector 27, and then a relationship with interior designer Piers Cameron. But despite this she visited and spoke to Mercury almost daily, and he was never far from her thoughts. When she and Cameron had their baby boy Richard, it was Mercury, by whom Mary once hoped to have a child, who became the godfather and who lavished all manner of gifts on the tot. When his love affair with Mary finished, Mercury blamed it on the band's constant touring, saying that life on the road meant being open to 'all kinds of influences'. It was a typical Mercury euphemism for the male lovers that were to fill his sex life to the brim. Mercury's former personal manager Paul Prenter, speaking about the singer's powerful sex drive, remarked that there was more chance of Mercury walking on water than going out with a woman.

By his own admission Mercury was not an easy man to live with: 'I generate a lot of friction. I am not the easiest person to have a relationship with.' Nor was he, but Mary coped with the dramatic, high-spirited star better than most.

Many of Mercury's friends found his relationship with Mary strange. His first publicist, Tony Brainsby, said: 'When I first started working with Freddie, Mary was already with him. They seemed very close, but I always found it so odd because he was so gay. But Mary helped Freddie a great deal. She would help him with his clothes and stage gear and do his make-up for him. She seemed invaluable.' Tony Pike, owner of the gorgeous hotel on Ibiza which Mercury fell in love with in the mid-eighties and visited regularly from then on, commented on the other hand: 'Mary was with him an awful lot and I could understand it. It didn't seem odd to me. I know a lot of men who seemed straight – they were even married and had kids – who then turned gay,' while according to Peter Straker, a long-time friend of Mercury's, 'Freddie and Mary absolutely adored each other. There was no doubt about that.'

What puzzled many people about Mercury and Mary's relationship was that she did not easily fit into the stereotypical roles that women usually play when they are close to gay men. But then Mercury loved to boast that he never did anything normal and his relationship with Mary was certainly no gay cliché. She wasn't a 'beard', a pretend girlfriend that a gay man brings out to hide his homosexuality and to appear straight. Neither was she a 'fag hag' – the kind of woman gay men like to have around them but for whom they have no really deep feelings. No, their relationship was, according to Mercury's inner circle, as close as any Mercury had with his male lovers – though its sexual flame had been extinguished long ago.

Mary provided the star with security without hampering his freedom and his promiscuity: whenever he needed her she was always there for him. And it was not just on an emotional level that their relationship worked. In the beginning, close friends say, it was Mary who encouraged and abetted Mercury's flamboyant dress sense, showed him how to apply make-up and the black nail varnish that was to become his trademark in those early Queen days – all vital to creating out of Frederick Bulsara, the seller of second-hand clothes, Freddie Mercury, the preening and posturing showman of rock.

Mercury once said: 'Mary and I will probably grow ancient and grey together. I can't imagine life without her. Sometimes a good friend is much more valuable than a lover.' It wasn't a flash quip of the kind that Mercury normally made when questioned about love and those close to him – the kind of elegant *bon mot* that got him out of a difficult spot. For it was truer and more honest than most of his outrageous answers. He and Mary might well have 'grown ancient' together if AIDS hadn't stopped him from growing old disgracefully.

The other woman in Freddie Mercury's life was a big-busted German actress with three ex-husbands to her name. Mercury met Barbara Valentin when he moved to the Bavarian town of Munich because he felt life in London was getting too claustrophobic. In Munich, with its easy-going atmosphere and vibrant gay scene, he could do exactly what he liked without the worry of censoring or prying eyes.

Mercury and Valentin crossed paths by chance in a homosexual bar called New York and they were immediately taken with each other. The singer found Valentin, who was popular on the gay scene because of her work with German film director Rainer Werner Fassbinder, immensely fascinating and she fell equally for Mercury's charisma and *joie de vivre*.

That first meeting resulted in Mercury accompanying the buxom actress into the ladies toilet, where they chattered away without being disturbed by the noise of the bar or the din of the disco. As Valentin sat on the toilet seat, Mercury crouched beside her on the floor, a glass of his favourite Russian vodka in his hand. Here they talked about their lives like a couple of long lost friends. Speaking from that Munich flat she and Mercury shared, the talented actress (who has made over seventy films) told me of their first meeting: 'It was a complete accident. We just happened to be in the same bar. He was with a big crowd and I was with a big crowd. I burned one of his friends with a cigarette accidentally and he shouted at me. Then he said sorry and asked if I would like to have a drink with his friend – that friend turned out to be Freddie.'

'We said hello to each other and that was it. For the next twenty-four hours we hardly stopped talking. We spent hours in the toilet talking because it was nice and quiet, and then afterwards we went home to my place and carried on chatting. He even called his boyfriend in the middle of the night from my place to let him know where he was. We talked about everything. I told him about my life and he told me about his. I found him mesmerising and just fascinating.'

They reminisced fondly about their past, talked about their loves and losses and their hopes for the future. When they finished talking Barbara Valentin opened the toilet door and the two of them walked hand in hand back into the bar to find it deserted and locked up. It was four o'clock in the morning and they had been gossiping away for almost half the night. They stayed talking to each other until the cleaning lady arrived a few hours later and let them out.

It was the beginning of a beautiful, if strange, friendship. Much later Valentin was to say: 'Freddie and I didn't have a normal relationship. He was gay and I liked men. But we were in love.' Their fondness for each other was such that they even bought a flat together, which they shared until Mercury decided that three years in Munich was enough and went back home to London.

During those three years he and Barbara became inseparable. When I interviewed him at a party in Munich to celebrate the release of Queen's *The Works* album, she was there too. He pointed her out to me, saying: 'See that big-titted girl? That's Barbara. She was once the Brigitte Bardot of Germany. She's such a laugh.' She was, too. If Mary Austin was shy and retiring, Barbara was the exact opposite. Like Freddie, she believed in living life to the limit. They would cruise the gay bars of Munich together as Mercury drew men towards him like a magnet. Sometimes Barbara, Mercury and his new conquest would all end up in bed together, while at other times each would get jealous of the men the other was attracting. On one occasion Mercury hit a man he felt was paying Barbara too much attention.

But for the most part their night-time sorties were pure decadent hedonism. One of Mercury's party pieces according to Valentin was to invite a pride of beefcakes back to the flat, get them to take all their clothes off, dress them up in women's hats – cloches, feathered concoctions and mysterious veiled numbers – and then sit them all down in front of the television. Then the singer would put on a video of one of his favourite films, *The Women*, and scream with delight when one of the actresses appeared on screen wearing a hat rather like one of those he had plonked on the naked young men's heads.

Valentin, who still looks seductive at fifty, said that Mercury had an unquenchable sex drive and went for men with large faces and big hands – what she called 'lorry-driver types.' Some men were just flings lasting a few hours; others, like a German bartender with whom Mercury exchanged wedding rings, were more serious lovers. But Valentin believes that despite the army of men in his life, the love they shared was deeper and more devoted than any of his Munich dalliances. After his death she told German magazine *Bunte*: 'I wasn't jealous as such. I always spent much longer with him than anyone else.'

Sometimes the vivacious actress would get upset by the 'rough trade', the coarse gay clones for whom Mercury had a penchant. She told him that a man of his intellect, wit and charm shouldn't fool himself into thinking any of them was Mr Right or a body-beautiful Einstein. Valentin recalled: 'He thanked me and admitted: "Barbara, without you, I would go to the dogs."'

'Sometimes the men he fancied were so stupid,' said Barbara 'some of them didn't have much more than a primary school education. I would tell Freddie, if you could understand how dumb they were you would be amazed. He would jokingly tell me to get lost and confess he didn't want to have a deep conversation with them, but just to go to bed with them. That was all. He enjoyed one night stands and affairs because they were easy and uncomplicated.'

Sometimes their involvements with other men could cause scenes. Barbara told me: 'One time this guy started washing my hair in one of the sinks behind the bar of a club we were in and Freddie got jealous and hit him. Another time I was flirting with someone else and Freddie got upset and slapped me. But to me that slap was like a bunch of roses. It was strange and different. But then our relationship was hard to understand, and I don't expect anybody to understand it.

The couple enjoyed themselves all over the world. In Rio, where Queen were headlining the prestigious 'Rock In Rio' festival, with Barbara's help Mercury stripped a security guard totally naked and threw his uniform out of the hotel window into the swimming pool below. The guard had come into Mercury's luxurious hotel suite merely to enquire if everything was to the singer's satisfaction and ended up caught in the mayhem that Mercury could conjure up at a moment's notice. As he stood naked before the couple, Mercury giggled and said: 'Oh well, that's rock and roll.' But such was the singer's sheer charisma that instead of knocking the Queen star's goofy front teeth out, the bemused guard joined the showman and the actress for a drink.

At other times it was Mercury who took off his clothes, Valentin says, and slipped into her dresses and high-heeled shoes, becoming an exotic drag act in the privacy of their million-pound flat, an act more flamboyant than anything he ever performed on stage. The actress also found a Jekyll and Hyde quality in the singer. Sometimes Mercury would fly into such a rage that he would throw his beautiful furniture around, his voice booming louder than during any microphone-enhanced performance. In an hour it would all be forgotten and he would be planting a rose with his delicate, womanly fingers or talking to the begonias in a caressing whisper. One such mood swing almost resulted in Mercury seriously injuring himself as, gripped in a kind of trance, he began beating his head against a radiator till both were covered with blood. Another time Valentin had to be rescued by her assistant when Mercury began to strangle her in his sleep. 'Freddie had no idea he was doing these things,' she told *Bunte* later. 'It was as if he was in a trance.'

But mostly Valentin saw the singer's gentle and caring side. 'Freddie was basically a very romantic person. He often put on an act as a hard, gay butch man but that wasn't the real him. He was good, gentle and very human. And he knew what was right and what was wrong. He helped so many people, there wasn't a mean bone in him. Many people in his profession and with his fame and success would have stuck the knife in your back as soon as you turned around, but that is something Freddie never did. He wasn't two faced.'

'Sometimes he would get very lonely and he would tell me how he hated being alone. At times like that we would tell each other our problems deep into the night. Whenever I told him my problems he was so attentive and concerned, though sometimes it was his humour more than anything that would help me. He would tell me I was being a stupid girl and to f*** off and come to my senses. And he was always right. We could just talk and talk and talk.

'He could be so attentive of me. One time I was ill and he just wouldn't leave my side. I begged him to go out and I found it hard to sleep because he was watching me so devotedly, but he refused to leave me there on my own.'

When he was in Munich one of his cats he had left behind in London had to have an operation and died afterwards. Freddie was out of his mind and just broke down into floods of tears. He flew home straight away the next morning for the cat's funeral.

'And in London last summer one of his beautiful golden koi carp was ill and Freddie's boyfriend Jim tried to heal the wound but was unsuccessful. In the end he had to kill the fish because he felt it was in such pain. Freddie and I were talking when Jim came in and told Freddie what he had had to do. Can you imagine, Freddie started to cry because of the carp, the tears just streaming down his face.'

In 1985 everything changed when Mercury suddenly decided to quit Munich and return to London. He gave the distraught actress no reason for his sudden departure, but she wondered why Freddie no longer wanted to stay in a city where he had so much fun. 'I knew there was something wrong with Freddie five years ago,' she said after his death. 'I knew he had AIDS.' In London the once-flamboyant singer turned into a shrinking violet, preferring the company of his flowers, cats and koi carp to partying, cruising and sex. He had become a ghost of the man who had mesmerised Valentin in that gay Munich disco.

In 1987 the couple were reunited when Valentin came to see Mercury perform his operatic duet 'Barcelona' with Montserrat Caballé. Valentin was horrified, she said, to see a dark patch forming on his face. The actress, many of whose close friends had died of AIDS, knew it was Kaposi's Syndrome, one of the signs of the fatal illness. 'I felt the earth shudder. I looked at Freddie and he looked at me. We didn't speak about it, but I knew the truth.

'After a few minutes I told him that he couldn't go on stage like that and put make-up over the dark blemishes on his face.'

In the following months the patches spread to Mercury's nose, throat, shoulders, legs and feet. Like his first girlfriend, Austin, Valentin confirmed that he was in terrible pain and had to resort to painkillers, but that he never complained about the agony he was in.

There were also visits to hospitals, made in the utmost secrecy – one of which was for a blood transfusion, Valentin claims. And in the midst of all this Valentin and Mercury visited a church in Switzerland, where they knelt down together and prayed for the miracle that was never to come.

Mercury enjoyed the visits from the friend he had once been so close to, telling others that he loved to see Barbara because she made him happy again. The summer before his death, on her last visit to him, Mercury played Valentin Queen's 'The Show Must go On' the last single the band released before the singer, died. It was released in October 1991. He was lying in his king-sized bed, looking dreadfully thin and gaunt. She sat on the bed and they reminisced about old times and looked through the photographs they had taken of each other, which Mercury had kept stored in a shoe box in a bedroom cupboard.

Mercury, who could once do without sleep for days on end, was now frail and tired and Valentin saw in his face the signs of his approaching death. She left the house with tears in her eyes, knowing they would never share any more happy times together. A few weeks later she sent him a key, made out of eighteen-carat gold, to the flat they had once shared – a key to a past he would never be able to revisit.

Chapter 9

MERCURY . . . AND OTHER STARS

Collaborations of Music and Dance

'Talent will out, my dear'

Freddie Mercury was gregarious, ambitious and easily bored. It was a perfect formula to produce a large canon of work, especially in collaboration with other artists. The singer loved the company of the big names in the entertainment world and many were frequent guests at his parties. Though he believed in being number one and though he wanted to be the best rock star in the world, he never saw his rock rivals as a threat, but rather as a catalyst to take his career down new avenues. Mercury was a restless worker, and that is why he did so much recording outside Queen, including his own solo efforts. He also got involved in a number of collaborations, his most adventurous being with the Spanish opera diva Montserrat Caballé, while his two most interesting pop fusions were with the ever-changing David Bowie and the reclusive Michael Jackson.

Queen and Bowie got together in Switzerland, where both spent a good deal of their time, to record 'Under

Pressure' in the group's beautiful Mountain studios, where the band had been working on their *Hot Space* album. It was a dance-based track with one of the most hypnotic bass riffs ever and it hit the number one spot in Britain in November 1981. Nine years later another version of 'Under Pressure' was back at the top of the charts when rapper Vanilla Ice borrowed the riff to interweave through his million-selling hit 'Ice Ice Baby'. The collaboration with Bowie was a complete accident, as Mercury told me: 'That record came about by pure chance, my dear. David came in to see us one day in the recording studios we own in Montreux, where we were working. We began to dabble on something together. It happened very spontaneously and very quickly indeed, and we were both overjoyed by the result.

'It may have been a totally unexpected thing, but as a group we are all strong believers in doing things which are unusual, not expected of us and out of the ordinary. We never want to get into a rut or become stale as a band and there is a danger of doing that when you have been together as long as we have. There is a danger of resting on your laurels and just getting lax and there is no way any of us would want that.

'David was a real pleasure to work with. He is a remarkable talent. When I saw him play in the stage version of *The Elephant Man* on Broadway, his performance fuelled me with thoughts about acting. It is something I may do in the future, but right now I'm looking at other projects to do within Queen. We never want to stay still. There are so many vistas to explore.'

Bowie, one of the rock world's most chameleon-like performers, had bought a home just outside the peaceful little Swiss town of Montreux so that he could get away from the reckless, drugs-oriented life style that had almost destroyed his career. 'Queen turned up in town and I went down to the studio to see them,' he told me. 'We just started to jam together and that led to a skeleton of a song. I thought it was quite an interesting tune; they liked it too, so we finished it off. But it was a real rush thing. It was done in about twenty-four hours, no more. It would have been nice to have spent longer on it.'

Mercury and Jackson worked on several songs together but, unlike the Bowie collaboration, these were never to see the light of day, lying hidden instead in record vaults. 'We had three tracks in the can,' Mercury told me, 'but unfortunately they were never finished. They were great songs, but the problem was time. We were both very busy at that period and never seemed to be in the one country long enough to actually finish everything completely.' One of the songs the pair, both relentless perfectionists, worked on was later to become Michael Jackson's duet with Mick Jagger, 'State Of Shock'. They worked together over a period of four days in Jackson's Los Angeles studio. It was an odd match: while Mercury loved sex and drugs, Jackson was a complete innocent in both these rock staples. To keep himself going during the sessions Mercury would snort cocaine, at first in the toilets to avoid upsetting the extremely religious and childlike star, to whom drugs, alcohol and cigarettes were all anathema.

Mercury and Jackson got together after rock's weirdest star saw a Queen show in Los Angeles. 'He used to come and see us all the time,' Mercury told me, 'and that is how the friendship grew. We were always interested in each other's styles and I would regularly play him the new Queen album when it was cut and he would play me his stuff. In the end we said: "Why don't we do something?" I should be kicking myself. I was going to be on *Thriller*.

'It was great to work with him as we had been friends before and that made it much easier than going into a studio and starting from scratch with someone you didn't know. One of the songs was something called "State Of Shock". Michael even called me to ask if I could complete it, but unfortunately I had to tell him I couldn't because I had commitments to Queen, so Mick Jagger took over instead.

'It was a shame, but ultimately a song is a song. As long as the friendship is there, that is what matters.'

Mercury made a host of 'secret recordings' which were never released for public consumption. One of the most surprising was with Wayne Eagling, the former principal dancer with the Royal Ballet, who was a close friend of Mercury's and persuaded the singer to perform a ballet on stage. Eagling choreographed the ballet scene in the band's *I Want To Break Free* video. 'Freddie would often come to see me perform at Covent Garden,' he said, 'and I would often see him on stage. We became good friends. We even recorded a gentle rock number together called "No, I Can't Dance". It was a terrifying ordeal for me having to sing it – all I could hear was my heart beating. But it was great fun to work on something like that with Freddie and I have still got that cassette of "our performance" together.'

Eagling says that Mercury was constantly dreaming up new ideas, his live-wire mind always working overtime on future creations and collaborations: 'One of the ideas was for us to do a spoof video which would include all the world's greatest ballet dancers, including Nureyev and Fonteyn, at a disco.' That would have been something else, had it happened.

A former sixties pop heart-throb was the only person at Freddie Mercury's bedside when the singer finally died after his long and brave fight against AIDS. Dave Clark, one-time leader of a North London band called the Dave Clark Five, had been a close friend of the singer's since the mid-seventies and visited the Queen star constantly, especially during his last tragic months.

It was not quite the death scene that Mercury might have wished. To have been surrounded by a body of his closest friends, all toasting his last few minutes on earth with the finest champagne and caviar, would have been a scene better suited to the theatrical star – an exit worthy of a true pop monarch. Instead, it was to be a very quiet death. But then, though all his closest friends knew Mercury was losing his battle against AIDS, they did not expect the end to come so suddenly. Many of them, including Clark, believed he would see another Christmas at his gorgeous London home.

So it was that Mercury died without some of his closest friends around him – his loyal valet Peter Freestone, his cook Joe Fanelli, his boyfriend Jim Hutton, his ex-girlfriend Mary Austin, his manager Jim Beach, the rest of the band and one of his oldest friends, Peter Straker. There was no family either; though the singer's parents, Jer and Bomi Bulsara, dashed from their Feltham home to Kensington as soon as they heard the news. Nor was there a doctor:

one had just left Mercury's bedside a few minutes earlier.

Only another pop idol, although one from an era long gone by, was there, holding Mercury's paper-thin hand, when he breathed his last. Dave Clark had scored a string of huge hits in the sixties, including the chart-topping 'Glad All Over' and 'Bits And Pieces', which reached number two, as his band spearheaded a London challenge to the Liverpool invasion of the Beatles and Mersey beat. Clark, born in 1942 in Tottenham, North London, was a former film stuntman, with dark gipsy looks. The band was formed when Clark was just sixteen years old, though they had to wait until 1963 for their first taste of fame, when they covered an obscure black rhythm and blues hit by the Contours called 'Do You Love Me?', which made number thirty in the charts of that year.

Clark did well out of the pop scene, scoring numerous hits, but he always had an ambition way beyond music. He was determined not to remain a mere pop relic eking out a meagre living, like so many of his colleagues from that era, when the music world decided it had had enough of him. At a time when numerous pop stars were' ripped off left, right and centre, Clark proved to be an incredibly astute businessman, and today he is a millionaire living in a beautiful apartment in London's Mayfair. His business acumen showed itself early on in his career. In 1967 the group decided to form its own film company, Big Five Films, making movies and documentaries, one of the first being about their own pop success.

Clark even embarked on an acting career, training at the prestigious Central School of Drama, but then realized his forte lay more on the business side. He got involved in music publishing and pop management, but one of his master strokes was buying the rights to one of the best British pop programmes ever, 'Ready Steady Go', which he and his band regularly appeared on. Clark grew richer and richer, operating wheels and deals behind the scenes, till 1986 saw him back in the limelight with *Time*, a spectacular West End musical which he had devised and written himself.

Clark, still a handsome man, speaking from his office in the heart of the West End, told me: 'I was the only one with Freddie when he died. It was very peaceful, but not expected at all. His doctor had only left about three minutes before and if he felt that Freddie was about to die he obviously would have stayed. None of us expected it; it just happened. It was still a shock to us all because it happened so quickly. I think Freddie still could have been here at Christmas.

'I think anyone who is about to die naturally wants to be surrounded by their friends, but really no one thought Freddie was going to die then. If we had known that Freddie had only hours to live his parents would have been there by his side. It was all totally unexpected.'

Clark says Mercury retained his dignity right until the very end: 'Freddie was very brave and he was determined not to be a burden on anyone. He was independent up until the end. Freddie fought against his illness with such strength and he never gave up hoping and praying that he would be OK. And it was marvellous the way that he carried on working.'

The day before Freddie died he announced to the world in a written statement that he had AIDS. Clark refutes claims that Mercury only made the statement because he knew he had merely a short time to live, and the entrepreneur also expressed anger about 'friends' who were never really close to the star in his final years but who talked about Freddie after his death, claiming they knew him up until the end: 'Freddie felt the time was right to put out the statement because of increasing speculation about his health. It was untrue of people to say he did it then because he expected to die the next day. That is just complete rubbish. He had no idea when he was going to die. It was a very courageous statement for Freddie to put out, but he did it because he was concerned for his family and friends and felt it was his own responsibility to talk about his illness.

'He did everything his own way and the statement was written by him. Right up to the end Freddie was in control of his own life. And Freddie could have been with us for weeks or months.

'One of the things Freddie wanted very much to do was to take away the stigma from AIDS and he felt that long before he died. He even took part in an AIDS benefit show for the Terrence Higgins Trust in April 1988 at the Dominion. 'No one should tell a person how to behave, especially at a time like that. He had to think not just about himself, but about everyone around him. For me that statement was very courageous, and said it all. I think it would have helped a great number of people an awful lot. Also there were one or two folk who made comments about Freddie when they had not even seen him for years. It was wrong, sad, and it was very hurtful for his friends and family.'

Clark also dismissed reports that the singer's home had been turned into a hospital and said whenever he visited it there were no nurses and no medical equipment there.

It was at the spectacular open-air concert at London's Hyde Park in September 1976 that Clark first met Mercury and Queen. 'I was invited by Queen to the concert,' he recalls, 'and I watched the show from the side of the stage. Afterwards we went for a Chinese meal at Mr Chows.

'I loved Freddie's work and when we got together we just hit it off. I met him at different functions and parties, but we only became really good friends after working together in the studio.'

That collaboration came about when Clark, impressed by Queen's front man, invited Mercury to write some tracks for his *Time* musical in 1985. It was the first musical Freddie had worked on and he wrote the eponymous title track, which was released as a single and reached number thirty-two in the UK charts in the summer of the following year. 'I respected what Queen had done,' says Clark, 'and I thought Freddie was going to be hard work, but he was the easiest person to work with. Yes, he was a perfectionist, but he could always take direction. He was incredibly hard-working. He would start at six P.M. and go right through until six A.M. And everything he did was like a perfect performance. Even in the recording studio he would sing as though there were thousands of people watching him, just like there had been at Wembley. He gave every ounce of energy and he never held back – he gave his all. Freddie always gave a performance which would give you goose bumps.

But although Freddie enjoyed writing for the musical he did not have ambitions to star in the show. 'Freddie said he could do three nights a week,' according to Clark, 'but he did not think he was disciplined enough to do eight shows. But he told me that he would definitely get up there one night and sing a couple of songs, which is exactly what he did when we had a benefit for the Terrence Higgins Trust.'

There was another side to Mercury, too, recalls Clark, a side the public never really got a chance to see: 'That was the kind, caring and generous one. In private Freddie was very different from the outrageous performer you saw on stage. He was so thoughtful. When we were recording in the Abbey Road studio he used to bring in a big hamper packed full with exotic foods including caviar, salmon, different cheeses and his favourite Cristal champagne. In private he really was a lovely and caring man. And his generosity went far beyond his closest friends and fellow workers. Total strangers regularly benefited from his kindness.

'If something came up on TV about someone in financial trouble he would send off a cheque anonymously through one of his companies. I remember him sending a cheque off to a couple who were out of work and whose house had been repossessed. He did things like that so many times. He would see something on the news or be told about someone's hardship and immediately reach for a chequebook. He liked real people. He may have been larger than life and one of the world's best performers when he was on stage but in private he was very, very human. It's the old story of the comedian who makes everybody laugh on stage, but off stage has a lot of sadness and sensitivity. You must never believe or be taken in by the image.'

Clark attended a number of Mercury's extravagant parties, including the birthday one in Ibiza in 1987. He was one of the close circle of friends flown in on the private jet that Mercury had hired. 'Freddie had got around a hundred and fifty extras in outrageous costumes to mingle among the guests and serve drinks. One person had a bird's cage on their head with real birds inside. It was absolutely amazing – something straight out of a movie set. Freddie was really dressed up too. I think he was wearing a very bright Hawaiian shirt.'

Clark was also at Mercury's famous hat party in 1986, where even the desserts masqueraded as millinery. 'It was a beautiful day and everyone had to come to the party wearing a hat. There were the most outrageous creations, the kind you would normally associate with Ascot and Gertrude Shilling. What made it even funnier was that all the waiters Freddie had hired were Chinese. I wore an Australian hat with all the corks hanging off it.

Nothing was too much trouble or too much expense for Freddie when it came to giving a party. 'For one birthday (about three years ago) Freddie flew over several chefs to prepare a meal which had twenty-five or thirty courses. It was served beautifully on this long table in his house. He was a great host and he really knew how to enjoy his money, which he shared with a lot of people. He was a perfectionist even down to his dinner parties. It was quite wonderful.'

'There were two sides to Freddie,' says Clark, '– the public and the private man. Freddie on stage was larger than life. He enjoyed the parties, he was a connoisseur of good food and wine, but he would not do anything he did not want to do.'

It was Clark who brought him together with Sir Laurence Olivier: 'I worked with Olivier on *Time* and he came to dinner at my house. One day he was listening to the album when Freddie's song came on.

'Olivier immediately said: "There's an actor for you" without knowing it was Freddie. I told Freddie this and he couldn't believe that one of the world's greatest actors had said that about him. He was as thrilled as a small child. Soon afterwards I phoned up Larry and asked if he would like to meet Freddie and then arranged a small dinner party for six. Freddie arrived at my house before Larry and he was a little nervous. But when Larry arrived with Lady Olivier they hit it off straightaway. Freddie had a wonderful sense of humour and was a great raconteur, just like Laurence Olivier – they just made you laugh.' Freddie was very well educated and well read according to Clark: 'Freddie was a great innovator. He loved the opera. He really was the first person to bring opera to the masses. Freddie was always very daring. To sing "Barcelona" with Montserrat Caballé was incredibly courageous. Freddie was a perfectionist at everything he did and would do a lot of research for every new project he attempted. Even videos were carefully and painstakingly thought out.

'Freddie did the whole storyboard for the video *I'm Going Slightly Mad*. I remember he poured through books on Cecil Beaton to get the colours exactly right. When you look at a lot of his videos he knew how to depict what was said in the lyrics perfectly. He knew exactly what he wanted, right down to the look and the lighting. He did most of the storyboards and he was well rehearsed before he performed in them. Freddie never stopped looking for new challenges.'

Mercury's adoring fans lost a true rock great, but Clark lost much more – a great friend: 'He was like a very rare painting. There will never be another Freddie.'

Freddie Mercury made a lasting impression even on people whose paths crossed his for the briefest of moments. One such person was one of the world's most ambitious and garrulous club owners, Peter Stringfellow, who has nightspots in both Britain and America. Fifty-two-year-old Stringfellow, dubbed by some as the oldest swinger in town for his jet-set raving, has seen the biggest names in the showbiz world pop into his clubs. One of them was Freddie Mercury. The singer made such an impact when he turned up at London's Hippodrome club, then owned by Stringfellow, that everyone stopped dancing, stared and then broke into applause. 'It was on our gay night and the word went round that Freddie Mercury was coming in,' Stringfellow, recalls. 'It was as if somebody had just said the King and Queen of Siam were about to honour us or the most important person in the world was due to walk in. The buzz went round and it was electric. Everyone stopped dancing and gawped at the balcony, where they heard he was going to materialise. When Freddie eventually walked in, he was in full splendour, dressed from head to toe in white satin, and the whole place just erupted and started applauding wildly.

'Everyone knew they were in the presence of a star and he knew they knew. He acted like a star, felt like a star and exuded a star's presence. He made the entrance at the Hippodrome as if he was going on stage. The only thing missing was the trumpets. It was theatre, pure theatre.'

When Stringfellow first met Mercury in 1972, it was a very different story. Mercury was then a fledgling singer and his name was not yet spoken in hushed tones on the gay circuit. But there was something about the singer that was to stay in Stringfellow's memory to this day – his vanity: 'He was just a nice kid then with long curly hair, but he did amuse me. We met in my club Cinderella Rockefellers and I said I'd like to take a photo of him. I'd got this Polaroid camera and we were having a bit of fun, so I said: "Let's capture the moment."' Mercury pouted and posed as Stringfellow took a few snaps. But every time the club host showed Mercury the result he cringed at what he regarded as an imperfect image and petulantly ordered Stringfellow to take a better picture. 'He posed in front of the camera, but it took ages,' says Stringfellow. 'In fact, I think I went through two films before he agreed to one photo which he let me keep for the club. He may have been fun to be with but he was deadly serious about the way he looked.'

After a swanky dinner at one of London's most exclusive restaurants, the Pontevecchio, a short walk from his home, Mercury would take care of the bill and then insist his whole dinner party come back to his place.

Once back at Logan Place, out would come the records and videos and he and his guests would listen to them for hours, talking and arguing late into the night about who was the best singer, and which star's performance was the most magical. But Mercury and his friends would not be discussing his rock rivals – the Mick Jaggers, David Bowies or Elton Johns – or the young pretenders to his rock crown. Instead the conversation centred around the opera and ballet greats with whom the singer had become obsessed. Lining the walls of his splendid home were shelf after shelf of opera and ballet videos and records.

One of the guests at these late night opera-ins was ballet dancer Wayne Sleep, who told me: 'Freddie was absolutely mad on opera and ballet. That's how I met him. He was very serious about it and knew so much about the art. He could talk for hours on the subject. He had thousands of opera videos in his home. He would put them on and then we would have fierce discussions about who was the best opera singer and who could sing higher than anyone else. It was just the kind of thing I would imagine opera buffs did after a few glasses of claret.

'Freddie was very knowledgeable about opera. He loved sopranos and he had an amazing voice himself. He also knew so much about ballet. Briony Brind was one of his favourite dancers. He loved going to the ballet and spent a lot of time at the shows. He went to everything.

'One of his favourite performances was *A Month In The Country*, which I starred in. In it Wayne Eagling and myself do *Swan Lake* together. There was also *Romeo and Juliet*, which was one of his favourite ballets. It was through his love of ballet and his frequent vists to it that I got to know him very well.'

Sleep believes that Mercury's operatic duet with the great Spanish diva Monserrat Caballé was just the start of something big and that he wanted to immerse himself more and more in the world of opera and ballet: 'His death was a tragedy because he was such a friendly, charming and talented man. But for me one of the most upsetting things about it was that Freddie had only just cracked the tip of the iceberg. He was the only pop singer to have done a duet with one of the world's greatest opera singers. And that was something he wanted to develop. It was, I know, the beginning of a whole new dimension. He definitely told me that was the area he wanted to go in.

'It was something he was already very involved in. We did a number of galas with Freddie and we also staged some of his numbers using classical ballet dancers. I think he would have ended up writing something for the Opera House or the Royal Ballet.'

It was his collaboration with Montserrat Caballé which most clearly signified to the public Mercury's embrace of the rarefied worlds of opera and ballet. It resulted in a hit album (*Barcelona* reached number twenty-five in the UK charts in October 1988) and a single of the same name, which soared into the top ten in November 1987. Mercury had written the song as the theme tune for the 1992 Olympic Games, which were being held in Barcelona, when the Spanish opera diva got in touch with him after she had seen him perform.

Much of his passion for opera was fuelled by his admiration for Caballé, whom he first saw perform at a concert in 1983. But it was only after Mercury revealed how much he adored the diva's singing on a Spanish television programme that she got in touch with him and suggested they should meet. 'After Montserrat watched the show she got in touch with me,' Mercury told me. 'The next thing I knew she was actually asking if I wanted to make a record with her. I was completely flabbergasted. Though I adored opera I had never thought about singing it. But after meeting Montserrat I've learned so much more about the music, and I have so much respect for it.'

Their first meeting was a terrifying prospect for Mercury, awestruck at the thought of talking to his idol: 'The first time we got together I was really nervous. I wasn't sure how to behave or what I should say to her. Thankfully she made me feel very at ease right from the start.' After a few further meetings he discovered that the two of them had a lot in common: 'I realised that both of us had the same kind of humour and that really thrilled and surprised me because up till then I had been labouring under the illusion that all great opera singers were stern, aloof and quite intimidating. But Montserrat was wonderful – after I told her I loved her singing and had her albums she told me she enjoyed listening to my music and had Queen albums in her collection too.

'She even thought I might ask her to sing some rock and roll and she was very game to try that too.'

The dream of recording a song with Caballé became a reality and grew more exciting for Mercury with each day that passed. 'Basically it all started out as one song, but somehow things just snowballed from there. Next thing I knew we were making an album together.' Initially, as he admitted to me, Mercury found it difficult to write music for opera: 'It was hard at first, as I was doing songs I'd never done before, especially written to suit our voices. It may have seemed rather ridiculous when you think of us both together, but the fact remains that we have something between us musically and so really it doesn't matter what we look like or what backgrounds we're from. The end product is the proof.'

The odd pop duo made their debut appearance together in front of six thousand fans at the exotic Ku nightclub in Ibiza, Spain, in May 1987. (Over the previous few years Mercury had fallen in love with this riotous, fun-loving island and had begun visiting it regularly.) The concert, 'Ibiza 1992', was designed to promote Spain's hosting of the 1992 Olympics in Barcelona. Singing 'Barcelona', accompanied by eighteen hand-picked musicians, Caballé and Mercury, in a dark dress suit and powder-blue waistcoat, were the highlight of the show.

Afterwards Mercury remarked: 'It was fantastic singing with her. What an experience! I have never written anything for opera or the operatic voice before. This really was a dream come true.

'Just before we went on stage I couldn't help wondering to myself if all this was really happening to me.

'And though I knew I was taking a big chance doing something like this it gave me such a fantastic rush that I can't wait to do more things like this.'

In October 1988 Mercury and Caballé performed at a star-studded show to launch Barcelona's successful bid for the 1992 Olympic Games at the Avinguda De Maria Cristina Stadium. I was one of the journalists who had been flown over from London to witness the spectacle. It was to be the last performance Freddie Mercury ever gave in public.

The extravaganza, which also featured Dionne

Warwick, Earth Wind and Fire and Spandau Ballet, was filmed for worldwide television and was attended by many famous names, including royalty. Among the 150,000-strong audience were King Juan Carlos, Queen Sofia and Princess Cristina, who all met Mercury afterwards.

But those who had come in anticipation of hearing the singer stretch his vocal range to the limit were in for a disappointment. Mercury was forced to mime his duet with Caballé after experiencing voice problems. It was then that more rumours started spreading in the pop world that all was not right with the flamboyant star. Earlier the singer had also been forced to abandon plans for a sumptuous after-show party at the city's Palacio de Perdrables. A spokesman for the star started at the time that the cancellation was the result of security precautions involving Britain's Queen Elizabeth II, who was due to stay there a week later.

Despite Mercury's fake performance, the show raised a lot of money and its profits went to the International Red Cross to help children suffering in war zones. Afterwards a disappointed Mercury commented: 'The atmosphere was amazing. It was just such a drag about my voice. Just as we were set to perform I started having difficulties, so I didn't want to risk singing live.' Later he was to add: 'I didn't really want to sing live because I felt we needed to have a lot of rehearsals behind us, which we didn't have time for. The songs are difficult and complex to do.' And of his meeting with Spain's King Carlos and his family he said: 'They were extraordinarily nice, especially the King, who made me feel completely at ease in his presence. He said how thrilled he was that I had written a song for the 1992 Olympics and told me he was certain it would be a massive hit.'

Caballé has wonderful memories of the time she spent with Mercury. In an interview from her homeland she spoke of his talent, kindness and generosity: 'He always used to say that my voice was like crystal and he used to send me boxes of expensive Cristal champagne to prove his words were true. He was so generous. He must have spent a fortune on champagne for me.

'I sent him in return one of my velvet and gold costumes, which he told me he had on display at his home.'

'In the time we spent together he was a real gentleman and always very kind to me. We developed a great friendship through our mutual love of music.

'Freddie loved all kinds of music, but he had a special passion for opera. I think he wanted to try and encourage more young people to appreciate the joys of opera and that was something he was able to do because he had so many fans out there.

'Our sessions together were such fun. Freddie would sit at the piano and play and I would sing by his side. I wanted him to sing opera himself because he had a great voice and a number of times I managed to coax him into doing just that.'

Caballé recalls how Mercury became a little worn out during their last recording session together: 'Freddie got a little tired, but I didn't think it was anything to worry about. Recording sessions can be draining, especially when they are so creative and productive.' The singer never told Caballé he was suffering from AIDS, but in one of their last phone calls he said he could not travel to Barcelona. 'Freddie thought it was too far for him to come and see me in Barcelona. But speaking to him on the phone he seemed in good spirits and very cheerful. I had no idea he was so sick.'

Mercury's passion for ballet manifested itself in his career and amounted to much more than the donning of leotards and pumps during stage performances. He believed ballet, like opera, could forge an interesting link with rock and offered a means of breaking down clichéd barriers and moving into new territories and dimensions.

After becoming friendly with many dancers in the Royal Ballet and with Sir Joseph Lockwood, a former chairman of the company, Mercury even performed with them in a charity gala. 'They had me rehearsing all kinds of movements and dance steps,' he recalled. 'There I was at the barre bending and stretching my legs. I was trying to do in a few days the kind of things they had spent years perfecting and, let me tell you, it was murder. At the end of it all I was aching in places I didn't even know I had.'

On stage during the gala Mercury's big moment came when he did his jumps and twirls while singing 'Bohemian Rhapsody': 'I did this very exotic leap, fell into the dancers' arms and they carried me across the stage as I was still singing. I still don't believe I did that. It was spectacular and the house went quite wild.

'I wasn't quite Baryshnikov, whom I absolutely adored, but it wasn't bad for an ageing beginner.'

Chapter 10

THE PUBLICITY GAME

PR and Freddie

'I don't like the way my teeth protrude.
Apart from that I'm perfect'

When Freddie Mercury first met Tony Brainsby he did not mince words. 'We are going to be the biggest band in the rock world,' he told the astonished publicist, 'and you can help us.' Then the wafer-thin young man with the finely sculpted face thrust his hands high in the air in a theatrical gesture better suited to a Victorian melodrama and let them slowly flutter down. When the hands finally came to rest by his sides, Mercury extended one to Brainsby in greeting. It was long and delicate and the fingernails, carefully manicured and painted with black nail polish, resembled not so much a part of the human body as a lovingly lacquered Japanese artefact.

Mercury, whose jet hair fell over the shoulders of his deep midnight-blue velvet jacket, was not a big-time pop star with a string of hits to his credit or a household name – his band hadn't released a record yet, and he and Roger Taylor still had a second-hand clothes stall in Kensington Market – and yet he behaved with more braggadocio than the most seasoned rock monarch. That first meeting totally convinced Brainsby he had in his presence a performer who would one day be truly famous.

Brainsby was then on his way to becoming one of Britain's top pop publicists. He told me: 'Freddie was a born star. As soon as he walked into the office I knew he was destined for stardom. You don't get that kind of feeling very often, but with him I knew. He was so very confident about Queen and their music. He knew exactly what he wanted them to become – not just in terms of sound, but also in terms of music.

'But I realised then that I was meeting a star, and that the band were going to be successful. Freddie already had the makings of someone larger than life. He was already very outrageous with his black nail polish and exotic clothes. He was quite camp and at the time it was quite a risk – especially as he did not have the safety of fame to explain away his majestic appearance.'

The fast-talking bespectacled publicity man turned up to see Mercury and his band in action at one of their first shows, at South Kensington's Imperial College, where Brian May was a student. He became a fan immediately, recalling: 'It was one of their first gigs. There was no stage for the band to perform on, and there were around a hundred people there, but they put on a great show. Freddie did the works. Your eyes were riveted to him. He knew how to hold and mesmerise an audience even then.'

Brainsby began attending more shows. 'One thing I could never work out,' he says, 'was that right from those very early days Queen had quite a massive following, and it wasn't just teenage kids. There were mums and grandmothers in the audience too. And to have that kind of audience when, in the beginning, they were basically a glam heavy metal band was absolutely staggering. It was so puzzling how they had such a big healthy cross-section of fans really from the word go.'

Brainsby found it easy working with the band because they were ambitious, had vision and were determined to succeed: 'For instance, photo sessions, which can be a nightmare for many bands who are unsure of their image or not confident about what they want to portray, were relatively easy with Queen.

'And interviews were larger than life too. There was an ordinary answer to a question and a Mercury answer which was always flamboyant and over the top.'

Mercury, though witty and outrageous in interviews, did not do many. 'He understood the pop game. He never wanted to fall into the trap of being over-exposed. He also did not want the spotlight to be on him and miss the rest of the group. He was determined to make sure that the band was all four members and not just Freddie Mercury and three other musicians. And he succeeded in that. It could have very easily been Freddie and the others, but it wasn't. Queen have always been regarded as a group.'

A couple of items were off the agenda in interviews and with the casual acquaintances Freddie met in those days: one was talk of his childhood, the other was homosexuality. 'He did not talk about his childhood or anything like that. His childhood was a closely guarded secret. I think he realised that the idea of a pop star who was born on the African island of Zanzibar and who was a Persian wouldn't be easily accepted by rock fans. There was no precedent for it.

And I never ever recall him saying that he was gay, but that didn't stop him camping it up outrageously. Every movement, every action was camp, and every sentence ended with a darling or a dear.'

One thing which fascinated Brainsby about Mercury was how classy he was: 'He was never vulgar, but he did like to have the best. One time the band were touring in America in the back end of nowhere and an ordinary taxi arrived to take Freddie to the airport. Freddie believed in travelling in style and using limousines, and though limousines would have been a rarity in that part of America, Freddie would not budge out of the hotel until a limousine was found. Eventually one was and Freddie arrived at the airport in the style that was to become a part of his life.'

Brainsby attended and helped organise a few of the Queen parties that were to become their way of life. 'One of the best was in New Orleans on Halloween Night. We hired out the hotel and turned it into a swamp complete with trees, creepers and fog, made by a dry-ice machine. It was a wild party. There were strippers and dwarves and one of my treasured possessions was a photo of Freddie signing one of the strippers' bottoms. Lots of people were very happy that night too, we had a special room with a couple of girls in it who were taking care of their carnal desires.'

Another spectacular bash was at Wimbledon Stadium, where around fifty nearly-nude models rode push bikes to publicise Queen's double A-side single 'Fat Bottomed Girls' and 'Bicycle Race' which were released in 1978. 'It wasn't really an official party, more a video shoot,' says Brainsby. 'We got around fifty girls to ride bikes all around the track. It was a huge success.'

Mercury was generous even in those early days.

According to Brainsby, 'He would spend a fortune on importing lorry loads of antiques even in the days when he didn't have a lot of money to his name. Freddie spent money like water. He had an immense amount of style – the things he bought were always very classy and upmarket. He was very generous, though he never gave me anything, but then there was no reason why he should. We weren't having an affair or anything!'

Mercury and Brainsby only ever had one row in the time they worked together and that was over Paul McCartney, another of the publicist's clients. 'That was the only problem we had,' remembers Brainsby. 'I had McCartney and Queen touring at the same time and I decided to go on the road with McCartney. I got a real rollicking from Freddie, who wanted me to be there with Queen, looking after them. That tour was pandemonium. I was dashing around the country like a mad man, going to the McCartney show, then jumping into a car and going to a Queen gig.'

When the band made 'Bohemian Rhapsody', Brainsby was one of the many who thought they had made a huge mistake: 'When I first heard it, though it was good, it was incredibly long. To start with I did think we had blown it. But Freddie proved everybody wrong. He really was a one-off talent.'

Another British publicist who played an important role in keeping Queen in the headlines was Phil Symes. Symes, who has handled many of the biggest names in show business, including Diana Ross, worked with the band for eight years, starting with their free concert in Hyde Park in September 1976.

'Freddie was both a flamboyant person and an

incredibly shy one,' he says. 'In public he was flamboyant. He loved giving parties – wild outrageous parties.
The atmosphere of them was always electric and
Freddie loved to be centre-stage at them. When a
lot of celebrities give parties they hide away in a
corner, but Freddie wasn't like that at all. He liked
to be out there enjoying himself and he wanted to
make sure that everybody else was too. He loved to
see people having fun.

'Above anything else he was incredibly generous.
When he invited his friends to the Munich party,
where everyone had to come in drag, he paid for their
air tickets and hotel bills. It was a huge spoof because
though all his friends were in drag, Freddie turned up
in men's clothes. I loved the Munich party. That was
such fun. The band's manager Jim Beach was dressed
up as Carmen Miranda and a whole host of names
including Steve Strange and John Reid were there.
Freddie often marked the occasion of one of his dos
by sending people photos of themselves signed with
a little message. There were some amazing ones from
that drag ball.

'But then after Freddie enjoyed himself at the parties
he went back to his very private life, where he was very
quiet and very shy. And that shyness is one thing that
a lot of people never realised about him because of his
flamboyant public image.

'He was especially shy in the company of strangers.
It always appeared that he had to get to know someone
before he could talk to them. But once he got to know
you, he was a very good friend. He had a very close
set of people around him, and those are the people
he would invite to his gatherings at home. He valued
loyalty very highly. And if anyone whom he embraced

into his circle sold stories about him he was always bitterly hurt by that. He felt that if he took you into his life, he expected that privacy to be maintained.'

The parties were not all bacchanalian revels. 'Some, of course, were wild, but most were nice and discreet,' says Symes. 'One would go around to his home, and it was usually people from the world of art, literature and fashion, all having these great conversations. He was very proud of his home and one of his greatest pleasures was showing people around it.'

Symes, like Brainsby, says that Mercury didn't like doing interviews: 'Basically he felt that the music said most of it, and he loved being private. And when he did interviews, for the most part, he became a performer again – he could be hysterically funny, camp, and he loved to create headlines. He loved being the showman and, let's face it, he was probably the greatest showman we've had in rock for years. His timing was great. He knew when to say something and how to say it. Everything, including the band's record releases, was planned down to the last meticulous detail.'

That artful planning, a belief in Queen's music and a burning ambition propelled Mercury to the top. 'I went with them to South America, where they were the first rock band to do a full tour,' says Symes. 'But then Freddie loved to do things first; he never wanted to come second. He loved being a winner.'

Although Tony Brainsby was the publicist in charge of the Queen account, it was one of his assistants, Chris Poole, who had most contact with the band. He travelled with them on the road, making sure their name was being brought to the attention of music journalists all over Britain.

Today Poole, one of Britain's most charming publicists, runs his own public relations firm with another press officer, Alan Edwards. They have a host of top names on their roster, including David Bowie and Prince. Poole recalls: 'Freddie was outrageous in those early days, though not as outrageous as he was later to become. He used to wear little fur jackets, black nail polish, and be very camp. But he was camp without behaving in a gay fashion. When Queen started it was just about the time when in London it was starting to be acceptable to be homosexual. Before then everyone was very closeted about the gay scene.'

When Poole first worked with Queen, Mercury was running a clothes stall in Kensington Market with Roger Taylor. At that time, at the tail end of the sixties, Ken Market, as it was known, was a hippy venue which attracted an odd mix of shoppers, dropouts, tourists and rock stars, who rummaged through its flower-power offerings and second-hand clothes. Attracted by its *ersatz* bohemian life style and the chance of a leisurely income, Mercury and Taylor decided to set up a clothes stall while they carried on playing in groups in their spare time. They paid £10 a week for the stall and aimed to buy up old clothes and restyle them into something new. Taylor's job was to scour junk shops looking for bargains. Occasionally they did good business, like the time Taylor bought a hundred overcoats for 50p each and sold them for £4 apiece even, so shopping legend has it, selling Mercury's own coat by mistake.

A former college friend, Tim Staffell, remembers how Mercury became more stylish after working in the market, replacing his jeans and white shirts with black satin gear, and how he shut down the stall when

Hendrix died as a mark of respect to his idol. After eighteen months the stall was shut down for good when the pair decided to concentrate on making music. Poole was not surprised: 'I went to the stall a few times and though it was fairly successful they didn't make a lot of money and were always broke. They sold the kind of clothes they liked to wear – lots of satin and velvet.'

When Queen first started to tour, Mercury was accompanied everywhere by his girlfriend, Mary Austin, who remained one of his closest friends all his life. 'I think they were very fond of each other,' said Poole. 'It seemed to me that she fancied him very much. And I think at that point he hadn't become completely gay. I felt from the very beginning Queen were going to be stars. But it wasn't just Freddie that was destined for success, it was all of them. Everyone always goes on about him, but the band in general were very bright and ambitious and they had something about them. You knew they were heading for the top.'

The band fell naturally into two camps: 'On one side was Freddie and Roger; on the other side was Brian and John. Though Roger was not gay, he and Freddie got on so well together. They were the ones who would sit at the back of the plane, where all the outrageous goings-on would happen, while Brian and John would be at the front.

'I had quite a good time with them, but they were not an easy band. On the first tour I did with them, when they supported Mott the Hoople, they were quite annoyed because they didn't get as much press as they figured they should have got. They may have been a support group, but they already had the mentality of big stars.'

Poole fell out with the band when he left PR to work as a journalist for pop paper the *Record Mirror*. He and the band did not speak to each other for eight years after he gave their second album a bad review. 'I didn't like it, slagged it off and they never forgave me,' he said. 'We didn't talk for eight years and it has only been in the last six years that they spoke to me again.'

Poole last saw Mercury at a party at London's exclusive Groucho Club to commemorate the BRIT Lifetime Achievement Award Queen received: 'Freddie didn't look horrible then, but he obviously wasn't well.'

Forty thousand feet up in the air Bryn Bridenthal and Freddie Mercury were rolling around on a large bed, giggling like schoolchildren, as the Lisa Marie made its stately way across America. The Lisa Marie was Elvis Presley's former plane, complete with its own private bed in the back cabin, and the band, obviously believing that what was good for the King was also good for Queen, had hired it during one of their successful tours of America. Even thousands of miles up in the air, fun never stopped for Freddie Mercury, who never believed there was a time and a place for anything, and for whom life's cardinal sin was being bored or being boring.

'He just grabbed me out of the blue, threw me on to the bed, jumped on top of me and we just rolled around together, laughing like crazy,' recalled Bridenthal. 'I felt as if I was twelve years old again and back at summer camp. But that is the effect Freddie could have on you. He could make you enjoy life the way a child does – unconditionally and with such zest.' Bridenthal was talking in her spacious

Los Angeles office, where she runs her independent publicity operation, originally bankrolled by Queen. For years she was the band's American publicist, travelling the world with them and enjoying their unreal life style. The vivacious PR, who now handles such top acts as Guns N' Roses, first met the band in 1977, when she was head of publicity at Elektra, Queen's American record label at the time.

'At that time a lot of people in the record company were not personally fond of the band, but I just fell in love with them,' she said. 'There were stories going around that it was difficult to hit it off with Freddie, but I never found that. He was just wonderful to me from the beginning. A lot of people in the record company just couldn't see it. They were always quizzing me about why I spent so much time with the band because they were impossible, but I never experienced that. I loved being with them. And frankly so many of those people in the record companies were so conservative, stereotyped and boring, if Freddie was intolerant of them, it was because he just didn't like wasting his time. Life was too precious for him.

'Freddie did not suffer fools gladly because a fool is a boring person and Freddie hated being bored. He told me that the worst sin in the world was being boring. When I look back now on those early months, one of the things that was truly remarkable was how Freddie, and all the other guys in the band, just accepted me. I went from being a total stranger to being close to them very quickly. You can never be sure why something like that happens, but I think they all realized how much I loved them and because of that they were willing to open up so quickly and reciprocate those feelings.'

Mercury was a complex character who even puzzled the people closest to him. He could be a totally outrageous show-off one minute, a shy, quiet introvert the next. If Queen's music was hard to label and pigeonhole, so was the man who sang it. Bridenthal, who got to know him as well as most, says: 'He was like a diamond, because he had so many sides to him, and all those sides were facets of his personality, and each of them was important to the sparkle. Off stage he could be as outrageous as he was on stage, but he could also be shy and quiet. They were both important aspects of his personality. At first I thought that the quieter times were times of renewal for him, but actually I realised it was much more complicated than that. He was both strong and vulnerable. He was a very complicated character.

'Sometimes when we would all go out to dinner he would dominate the table at the restaurant so completely, saying the most wonderfully funny things and telling such great stories. At other times he could sit quietly in a room and nobody would even notice him. The change in character was really amazing.'

Mercury had a rare talent: though he was ultra-intelligent, thinking about life never stopped him from enjoying it to the utmost. 'He would talk about life and the meaning of life to me,' says Bridenthal. 'We would often stay up all night chatting and he was always so interesting and fascinating. But equally he could gossip and just be frivolous. It was always entertaining, though often exhausting. There were times when I literally crawled out of his room on my hands and knees after we had been up the whole night.

'One of the things I really loved about Freddie, and which I thought was really smart, was that he never wanted to buy into the whole crap that often comes with being a celebrity. He wasn't the kind of person who had to go to the right places and be seen with the right faces. He never seemed to be interested in any of that and to me that was just evidence of what a quality person he was.

'He was a man who felt full and accomplished in himself which is why he was never taken in by the whole fame trip. A lot of performers get caught up in that, but that is because they are so empty inside; they feel that being a success can fulfil them, but it never can. What I always felt about Freddie was that he was his own person, and he had his own identity.'

Bridenthal got to know Mercury and the rest of Queen really well as she spent weeks on the road with them, evening after evening at restaurants and clubs, as well as accompanying them on their long jaunts overseas. 'One day I was sitting in the dressing room and the guys started changing their clothes in front of me. That's when I realised they were comfortable having me around them.'

Bridenthal accompanied the band on their ground-breaking tour of South America which started in February 1981. 'That was a trip of a lifetime,' she recalls, 'even if it did get rather hairy at times. When we were in Venezuela, a President had just died and it all got rather frightening. The country had so many upheavals and revolutions that for a time we all began to wonder if we were going to make it out of there.'

Though the stories of Mercury's promiscuity – especially in America – abound, Bridenthal believes he was more of a romantic than anything else: 'He was very romantic, definitely. He loved to be in love. But then he was basically a giver, and if you are a giver, the best thing in life that can happen to you is to have someone give you love back. Freddie was a very passionate person.' He also had a razor-sharp intelligence, and that was one of the factors that helped propel the band into the big time: 'He and the rest of the band didn't relish the idea of playing pubs and clubs and slogging their way around the country. They had a game plan, a bigger overview, and that was what they put into practice. They weren't building things year by year, gradually. That would have been too boring for them.'

One of Mercury's most complex traits was that though he could be incredibly open with friends, he wasn't that way in interviews. Bridenthal had a hard time getting Mercury to talk to the media, who plagued her constantly for audiences with the Queen figurehead: 'Freddie rarely did any interviews here. At the beginning he would maybe do one or two a year, but then that tailed off. I was always trying to persuade him to do more, but he wouldn't have it. Freddie hated to do interviews and I figured he hated doing them because he felt it was such a low common denominator. It wasn't challenging and it wasn't interesting to him and he just didn't like the idea of sitting with somebody who was trying to capture his essence in twenty minutes.'

One of the people crucial in getting Mercury to do interviews was Paul Prenter, his former personal manager and one-time lover, who was to die of AIDS a few months before the singer. Prenter was one of the few people who 'betrayed' Mercury when he sold his story about his life and times with Mercury to a British tabloid. His warts-and-all exposé of life with the star referred to the singer's rampant promiscuity and drug-taking. 'I must say Paul helped me get the interviews done,' Bridenthal says. 'When he left is when I stopped being able to get interviews with Freddie. But I will always wonder why Paul sold his story. It was such a mean-spirited thing to do. I was so surprised. Freddie was so good to the people around him, so generous and caring, that it seemed like the worst kind of person that would go against him and be disrespectful of the privilege of being close to him. I felt Paul hurt their career in America because he was so rude and so nasty to people so often. So when he and Freddie parted ways, I thought it was actually good and healthy for the band and their career in America.'

Bridenthal was one of the people who experienced Mercury's fabulous generosity first-hand. It was Mercury and the rest of the band who gave the PR the finances to start up her own independent set-up: 'They left Elektra, and so did I, and one day I decided to start my own company. It wasn't long after that I walked into the apartment I was renting here in Los Angeles to answer a phone call from the Queen office saying the band wanted to hire me as their independent PR. They wanted to bankroll my company and their manager Jim Beach told me it was one of the few things that all the band had ever agreed on. It made me feel so good.

'They were so generous to me too. As an independent they would always pay me in advance and every once in a while they would send me an extra cheque, so I was never stressed for money.'

Bridenthal realised that Mercury was ill a few years ago. Although most of the rumours about his sickness were doing the rounds in London, the gossip was also part of the Los Angeles rock scene. 'I thought I knew what was wrong with him,' she told me. 'I spent quite a bit of time with Brian because he was the one member of the band who spent more time here than the others. Every once in a while I would ask him about Freddie and he told me Freddie was having kidney problems. But Brian was a lousy liar and a sensitive guy and I knew it was more than kidney problems. But I felt that if Brian needed to lie to me about what was happening then that was fine. My feelings were: what was to be served by it, if it made him feel uncomfortable or if he didn't want to discuss it?'

Bridenthal paused for a moment as the memory of all the wonderful times she had with Mercury came flooding back: 'Whenever I hadn't seen him for a while, he would always rush over to me, give me a big kiss and hug and plenty of "darlings", and it always made me feel like a queen. Freddie had the ability to make me feel as if I was the most important person in the universe. Doing publicity is a crucial job in the rock world but, despite that, you're rarely made to feel appreciated. Yet Freddie made me feel more appreciated than anybody I have ever worked with in my entire life. That was his rare magic.

'He was so sweet and nice, totally different to the way you would expect someone of his stature to be. Yes, of course, he had temperament. What big star doesn't? But he never treated me disrespectfully. My memories of him all make me feel so warm inside. He had an incredible talent, but more than anything else he enjoyed life. He knew how to have fun. His death has left the world a much lonelier place. It was such a waste.'

Chapter 11

INNUENDO

Aids Rumours, Truths
– and Charities

'I don't expect to make old bones.
What's more I really don't care.
To live to seventy would be boring'

When Freddie Mercury walked into the Wembley TV studios at 10 a.m. on a cold February day to begin work on the video for the band's new single 'I'm Going Slightly Mad', the small group of people who had been employed to work on the promotion film froze with shock. The formerly chubby, muscly singer was a pale shadow of his former self. His clothes hung off his emaciated frame and his face, ravaged by blotches, was sickly grey in colour and very drawn.

Mercury had, in fact, only nine months to live. The video crew and technicians were told by the director that he might tire very easily and to prepare themselves for any delays and cancellations, but AIDS was never mentioned. Instead workers on the shoot of the last video that Mercury was to make were told that the singer had a knee problem and would have to take it easy.

Mercury himself told some of the crew: 'My knee has been giving me a lot of trouble and it means I have to rest from time to time.' A day bed was installed in Mercury's dressing room, which was guarded by two security men, where the frail-looking star would disappear to lie down.

But though AIDS or Mercury's poor state of health was never mentioned out loud during the gruelling three day shoot, a number of workers knew the star's tiredness was nothing to do with a wonky knee. One told me: 'I had lost a number of close friends to AIDS and Freddie looked just the way they did towards the end. He really looked in a bad way. It was like staring death in the face. Besides, that story about having a bad knee just didn't make any sense. During some of the sequences Freddie had to crawl furiously across the floor. If he really had a bad knee he just wouldn't have been able to do something like that. To me his knee looked the most healthy part of his body.'

So that his AIDS ravaged face wouldn't be seen on the screen, Mercury adopted a disguise of thick white pasty looking make-up and topped it off with a huge black fright wig. And to make himself fatter Mercury wore a long sleeved T-shirt under the suit that he wore in the film. No one watching the video would think it odd because the band often dressed up and the theme of this particular song was, after all, madness.

Freddie Mercury knew he had AIDS for five years, but he did not admit publicly to the disease until twenty-four hours before his death. Though he was a flamboyant showman, secrecy was always a part of his make-up and when Mercury learned he had AIDS he became more guarded than ever, only telling a handful of his closest friends and swearing each one of them to secrecy.

Such was his fierce determination to keep his illness under wraps that even the three other members of the band he had spent most of his working life with were not told until a few months before his death. Guitarist Brian May remarked just a few days after Mercury's death: 'It was always a private thing with Freddie. We knew instinctively that something was going on, but it was not talked about. He did not finally tell us until a few months ago. But certainly he knew for five years or so. He was living under a shadow for a very long time.'

May and Roger Taylor had decided to break their silence about Mercury's agony and death in an interview with British breakfast station TV AM, during which they praised his bravery in dealing with the illness and finally admitting that he had AIDS. May said: 'Freddie made the crucial decision to disclose he had AIDS. It would have been very easy for him to put on his death certificate pneumonia and Freddie knew that. He knew he could have sidestepped everything. But in the end he said: "I have got this, and there is no shame, no stigma."'

But if his fans learned he had AIDS just twenty-four hours before his demise, the showbusiness world had been buzzing with rumours for years, not months. Even at the beginning, when Mercury did not look the gaunt, spectral figure he was to become in the last two years, showbusiness mafia sensed something was wrong. After all, the singer had suddenly turned into the Howard Hughes of rock, hardly ever going out and making very few public appearances. It was a most odd state of affairs for someone for whom partying was in the blood, for someone who couldn't wait to throw his next bash. Mercury tried to shrug off his absence from the party scene by saying that he had grown old, and that he was tired of the same old faces. But his excuses had a hollow ring to them. He said that he now preferred to stay at home and tend to his garden rather than to rave.

The rumours that Mercury had AIDS first began in 1986 after reports that he had had a blood test at a Harley Street clinic. Mercury, just back from an extravagant shopping spree in Japan, was furious at the reports and said tetchily: 'Does it look as if I'm dying? I'm very fit and perfectly healthy. These rumours are just rubbish. They make me feel sick.'

But the rumours would not die down. When the singer lost his voice at the spectacular La Nit concert in 1988 in Barcelona the word that he was seriously ill started up again. A few days later, at a party at the Royal Opera House, he was fielding questions about his alleged illness. 'These rumours are complete rubbish,' he told me. 'It's true I've stopped nights of wild partying, but that's because I'm no longer a spring chicken. I just can't carry on the way I have done in the past. It's no way for a grown man to behave. But it's nothing to do with me being ill, it's simply because I am getting on. Besides, this is what growing up is about.' When I asked him why he hadn't thrown a huge bash for his recent birthday he replied: 'I just didn't feel like holding an extravagant do. This time I wanted something a little different. I fancied a much smaller and much more intimate gathering. Another big Freddie Mercury bash would have been perfectly tedious.'

Queen's manager Jim Beach claimed the change was

because Mercury had now reached forty and added: 'Freddie's life style has changed a lot. He has slowed down a great deal. Hitting forty is a watershed in any man's life and Freddie is no exception.' But two of Mercury's closest friends had recently died from AIDS and a source close to the Queen front man confided at the time: 'This has worried Freddie tremendously. Yes, he was wild, carefree and promiscuous once, but these days he doesn't want to run risks with his life. He doesn't see the point of going on any more.' And Mercury himself admitted that casual sex was no longer a part of his life and that he worried for young people, given the problem of AIDS: 'You can't expect people to just abstain from sex. But that's why I think the message of safe sex is so essential and crucial. Anyone who sleeps around should have an AIDS test. Once sex was so important to me. But now I'm totally different. I'm almost a nun. And everything is fine. I don't miss my old kind of life.' This was a very different Mercury indeed.

After the party for his Barcelona album, Mercury was to make one other public appearance. In February 1990 Queen were presented at the prestigious Brit ceremony with An Outstanding Contribution to Music Award. The music business workers saw how ill Mercury had become. He looked gaunt and haggard as he went on stage with the rest of the band to receive the award. Usually the band's spokesman, he stood meekly by as guitarist Brian May accepted the honour. His weight loss was attributed by close friends to part of a new fitness regime because, he said, he was concerned about being overweight. And his anaemic complexion was explained away by the fact that on that night he hadn't applied any stage make-up.

After that, sightings of Mercury became very rare, but at each one the singer looked worse and worse. Yet all the time Mercury was adamant that he was in fine health and his spokeswoman Roxy Meade insisted: 'Freddie is fine. He is perfectly healthy. There is nothing wrong with him.' And his Queen colleagues also constantly denied that their front man was ill.

In the spring of that year Mercury went shopping at the Chelsea antiques market in the King's Road for more of his treasured antiques, including some Art Nouveau pieces. Despite the warm weather he had wrapped himself up in a long woollen scarf. Again he was accompanied by his minder, now a permanent fixture by his side, and there to get rid of any unwelcome intrusions.

Now the rumours of Mercury's illness were multiplying. Mercury's representatives were rung every day as a new speculation or sighting occurred. But the chain of loyal friends that had formed a human barrier around the singer never broke. Always outsiders were told that there was nothing wrong with Mercury. 'He has just had a nice meal,' Roxy Meade would say, or 'He's just bought some new paintings.'

But the truth was that Mercury was dying of AIDS. In July of that year I already had written an obituary for my paper, London's *Daily Mirror*, one of the biggest-selling papers in the world. It started: 'Freddie Mercury was pop's most flamboyant superstar. The bisexual singer's life made Elton John look like a shy wallflower in comparison. On stage Mercury was an over-the-top performer full of grand, dramatic gestures, who camped it up mercilessly. Off stage he was little different. He loved wild living, riotous parties and spending money.'

The next month another new rumour was racing around the pop world – that Mercury had already died, that the singer was being buried secretly and that his death would only be announced after his burial. This was untrue and Queen's publicity people said that Mercury would lay to rest all the rumours in the next few days by saying he was very much alive. He never did and the rumours of his illness blew up once more.

At his London home, which had now become his sanctuary from the rest of the world, one of Mercury's staff claimed: 'Freddie is alive and well and eating his Sunday lunch. We will be taking legal action against the perpetrators of this rumour. Freddie went shopping on Saturday and will be going out shopping again this week.' But if the end had not yet come, it was not that far off.

Yet the knowledge that he had AIDS channelled the workaholic star into a frenzy of new recording. If he had died five years earlier he would have left a vast musical legacy, but knowing so far in advance that death was inevitable ensured that he could create even more magical music. He began embarking on projects that he had always wanted to see through and stockpiling a great body of work. Friends say that he was still working six weeks before his death.

Indeed it was at that time that he decided he had to do something to help fellow sufferers whose lives had been wrecked by the disease that was to end his own life, AIDS.

The AIDS charities were all in urgent need of cash to care for the thousands ravaged by the disease and to further research into a problem that was multiplying every year. Propped up in his huge bed, desperately battling against the inevitable end, the singer made up his mind that he must leave some money to one of these charities. To donate the profits from one of his most memorable songs was an idea that appealed to the dying star and the AIDS charity he particularly wanted to benefit was the London-based Terrence Higgins Trust, which had done much to pioneer the care and treatment of AIDS patients. It was not a straightforward decision, however, since the AIDS epidemic was far worse in America than in Britain and money was just as desperately needed there.

A few days later, the dilemma of who to give the money to was resolved out of the blue. The legendary American basketball star Magic Johnson, who once boasted of his heterosexual prowess, announced to the world on prime-time television that he had contracted the AIDS virus. He was setting up a foundation to try to tackle the problem and Mercury and a close coterie of friends and workers decided that this would be another worthwhile cause to benefit from the Queen coffers.

On 26 November, just two days after the singer's death, his dying wish was made public. The three remaining members of the band, Roger Taylor, Brian May and John Deacon, took the decision to re-release 'Bohemian Rhapsody', Queen's landmark hit. They announced that it was being put out as a tribute to the dear friend they had lost and that all the proceeds would be donated to the Terrence Higgins Trust, the British charity for AIDS. A few days later they made a further pledge that the profits from the American sales of the record would go to the new foundation set up by Magic Johnson. Queen's manager, Jim Beach, announced; 'We hope that by joining forces with Magic we can forge a link between music and sport and help to make it known – as Freddie wished – that AIDS concerns us all.'

The public responded magnificently. Just six days after 'Bohemian Rhapsody' was re-released, the single which assured Queen's place in the annals of rock history had stormed to the number one spot. As I write this the record looks poised to become the biggest-selling British single ever, even topping the three million copies that Band Aid sold with its Ethiopian famine charity song, 'Do They Know It's Christmas'. The Mercury tribute knocked another charity record off the top slot, Elton John and George Michael's duet of 'Don't Let The Sun Go Down On Me'. As the record claimed the top spot, Michael said: 'I am delighted that Queen have gone to number one. I was always a big fan of the band's and was very saddened by Freddie's death.'

The re-release of 'Bohemian Rhapsody' was achieved in lightning time. Every effort was made to set the wheels in motion as soon as possible after the singer's death. According to Tony Wadsworth, general manager of the group's record company, 'First copies in a picture bag were with us the following Friday. Everyone pulled out all of the stops.' And after a day it was obvious to everyone in the record industry that they had a monster-selling record on their hands. Graham Walker, from the chart research group ERA, said: 'Sales have been phenomenal. This is all set to be one of Britain's biggest-selling records. In the first six days we have estimated the record has sold around six hundred thousand copies.'

Even in his death Mercury was still the perfect showman. A month before the end Queen released one of their most poignant and moving songs, 'The

Show Must Go On', with its haunting lyrics which, though questioning the meaning of life, ultimately gave a message of hope and survival. Two weeks after the release of the single came the band's *Greatest Hits II* album, containing some of their most electrifying songs. Even in the midst of tragedy, everything seemed to be perfectly stage-managed – a fitting finale for a great showman who always knew how to make an entrance and an exit. Yet though his closest friends praised Mercury's bravery in fighting the disease, others in the pop world accused him of cowardice and of betraying the gay cause. They believed that Mercury should have admitted he had the AIDS virus a long time ago, and that the act of announcing it just twenty-four hours before he died was not courageous or heroic at all. Many felt that by not admitting to having AIDS earlier he made gayness and the disease still something to be ashamed of, still a stigma. They also pointed out how much money he could have raised by speaking truthfully and honestly about his situation and his fight against AIDS. Research expert Dr Roger Ingham from Southampton University said he regretted that Mercury had not told the world about his illness in the early stages as Magic Johnson had done: 'Maybe if Freddie Mercury had revealed his illness much earlier it would have brought discussion out in the open, and that would have been a very good thing.'

Shortly after Mercury's death I did an interview with Dannii Minogue, a new teenybop idol in Britain and one of the people who believe Mercury should have spoken out about his illness earlier. She said: 'His death was pretty sad. I wasn't a huge Queen fan, but I know some friends who were close to him and

I think it's sad he didn't announce about his illness earlier.

'Everybody could see what was happening to him; it was very obvious. It is a shame that he didn't admit exactly what was wrong with him. If he had everybody would have been so much more supportive of him. He should have done what Magic Johnson did and used it as a platform to spread the word about AIDS and raise money for it. Instead it just seemed that he was ashamed. When he finally announced about how we should fight against this disease in our midst it was a nice gesture, but I just thought it was a message he should have given ages before.'

But in the end it was a decision Mercury had to make on his own, whatever the rights and wrongs of his choice. And if he chose to cover up the facts it was because he knew that however hard it is to live in the limelight, it is even harder to die in it.

QUEEN CHRONOLOGY

1968 Brian May, a student taking a Physics degree course at Imperial College, London, places a handwritten note on the college noticeboard inviting other students to join him in forming a band. One of the first to do so is bassist and vocalist Tim Staffell, followed by drummer Roger Taylor. They call themselves Smile.

1969 An American label, Mercury, signs the group for a one-off deal. The result is 'Earth', a Tim Staffell song, which is released in America only and does nothing. The group are dropped from Mercury.

1970 Staffell leaves the group to join another called Humpy Bong. But he persuades a former fellow graphic art student, Freddie Bulsara (later Mercury), to join Smile. It transpires that Mercury has been living just up the road from May's Feltham home without ever meeting him. Mercury has previously sung for the groups Wreckage and Sour Milk Sea. In November the band, now called Queen, play Ballspark College, Hertford.

1971 So far the band have been without a regular bass player, but in February John Deacon answers a classified ad and joins them.

The same month the band play Hornsey Town Hall and Kingston Polytechnic.

From July to September the band embark on their first ever tour, playing throughout south-west England.

At the end of the year they play two concerts for friends at Imperial College, London, and a New Year's ball at Twickenham rugby club.

This year Queen get their big break. They are asked to give studio demonstrations of new equipment at De Lane Lea recording studios. Their reward is unlimited studio time, which they use wisely, making demos.

1972 Queen take a year off the road. This year they only play five shows – including one organised by Deacon to just six people – but among them is an important one at London's famous Marquee Club at the end of the year. Instead of slogging up and down the country they throw all their efforts into making their first album at Trident Studios with whom they sign a management, record and publishing deal. It is also the year Mercury designs the Queen crest.

1973 After their debut album, *Queen*, they are signed up by record giants EMI. They play the Marquee again in April. EMI intend the gig to launch the group.

In June Mercury, calling himself Larry Lurex, releases a single called 'I Can Hear Music'.

The following month Queen's debut single, 'Keep Yourself Alive', is released, amidst accusations of hype. Radio One refuse to put the single on their play list and it fails to chart.

Their debut album, *Queen*, released the same month, is followed by their second album, *Queen II*, which is recorded in August.

September sees a concert at the Golders Green Hippodrome, and the following month they play Frankfurt in Germany and the Paris Theatre in London, a gig which is recorded by Radio One. They also make an appearance on French and Dutch television.

In November they play Imperial College again and then embark on a tour supporting the hit band Mott the Hoople, with gigs throughout Britain.

Queen are starting to build a strong following.

1974 The momentum gathers. Queen appear on the bill at the Sunbury Music Festival in Melbourne, Australia, in February, and the same month their single 'Seven Seas Of Rhye' is released and reaches number ten.

In March Queen open at the Winter Gardens, Blackpool, the opening leg of their first headlining tour which ends up at the Rainbow in London on the 31st. Mercury is not surprised at this development. He says at the time: 'I've always thought of us as a top group.'

The same month *Queen II* is released and reaches number five in the UK charts.

In May the American tour is called off after Brian May develops hepatitis. The band return home and start work on their next album, planning their schedules so they can work around Brian's ill health.

In October 'Killer Queen', taken from their as yet unreleased third album, is released as a single and is a huge hit, reaching number two. The band play the Palace Theatre, Manchester, the opening gig of a UK tour.

The following month their new album, *Sheer Heart Attack*, is released and reaches number two, Queen embark on a short European tour.

1975 Queen start the year with a new release, 'Now I'm Here', which reaches number eleven. In February the band begin their first headlining tour of America in Columbus, Ohio. An added boost is being voted 'Band of the Year' by *Melody Maker*.

Mercury is diagnosed as having a throat virus, nevertheless, the group manage to finish the tour.

After a short holiday, the band are back at work again, this time with a tour of Japan.

In August the band split with Trident and decide to sign up with Elton John's manager, John Reid. According to Freddie, 'One leaves them behind like one leaves excreta.'

Meanwhile the group are busy recording *A Night At The Opera*, their new album.

At the end of October a track from the forthcoming album *Bohemian Rhapsody* is released. EMI are doubtful about the wisdom of releasing this lavish operatic pastiche, but it is leaked to one of Britain's top DJs at the time, Kenny Everett, who gives it a great deal of air play, creating a large demand.

In December the single reaches number one and stays there for nine weeks. The promotional video also makes its mark and starts the pop video revolution.

Meanwhile, Queen have been touring the UK again, opening in Liverpool in November and closing at the Hammersmith Odeon on Christmas Eve. This final gig is shown live in a special edition of the BBC's 'Old Grey Whistle Test'.

By the end of the year *A Night At the Opera* reaches the UK number one spot.

1976 In January Queen embark on another US tour, opening in Waterbury Palace Theatre, Connecticut.

The promotional tour pays off as 'Bohemian Rhapsody' hits number nine in America in April.

Queen consolidate their success by immediately following the US tour with a tour of Japan and Australia.

In June 'You're My Best Friend' is released and reaches number seven. The group go back to the studios to begin recording a follow-up album.

In September they play dates in Edinburgh and Cardiff and are a big hit at a free concert in Hyde Park, an enormous show attended by 150,000 people and broadcast live by Capital Radio.

In November 'Somebody To Love' is released and reaches number two, while the new album, *A Day At the Races*, released the following month, hits the top spot.

During the year Mercury has been producing Eddie Howell's 'Man From Manhatten', on which he also plays.

1977 This year starts with a tour of America supported by Thin Lizzy.

In March 'Tie Your Mother Down' is released, only reaching number thirty-one in the UK and forty-nine in America.

After returning from America, Queen decide to tour Europe and the UK, ending with two nights at Earls Court, staged in lavish style to the tune of £75,000. But the band prove unpopular with the British music press, who call Mercury a 'prat'.

In May Queen release their first EP, with lead track 'Good Old-Fashioned Lover Boy', and it reaches number seventeen.

Work starts on a new album, *News Of The World*, which is finished by September. The single 'We Are The Champions' is released and reaches number two, swiftly followed with a number four spot for the album.

In November Queen embark on an American tour, opening in Portland, Oregon. They stay in America until the end of the year.

Mercury's solo project this year is producing an album by one of his oldest friends, Peter Straker, called *This One's On Me*.

1978 In February the group release a single called 'Spread Your Wings', which reaches number thirty-four.

Queen continue to tour, this time with dates in Europe, ending with two days at Wembley. Afterwards, the band retire into the recording studio to work on their new LP, *Jazz*.

A single, 'Fat Bottomed Girls', is released in October, reaching number eleven, and another tour of America starts in Dallas.

On 10 November the LP *Jazz* is released, reaching number two. Queen continue on tour in America until the end of the year.

1979 This year kicks off with a European tour, during which 'Don't Stop Me Now' is released, reaching number nine.

The group move on to Japan in April for an extensive tour. The European dates are recorded and released as LP *Live Killers*. This reaches number three, but the sound quality is poor and Roger Taylor publicly denounces the LP. A single released from it, 'Love Of My Life', only gets to number sixty-three.

But in June and July Queen are back in the studio recording their next album, *The Game*, and October sees the release of a single, 'Crazy Little Thing Called Love', which Mercury says he wrote in the bath. It is a big hit, reaching number two in the UK, and a first number one for Queen in the USA, but, even more importantly, it receives acclaim from the critics – something the group have regularly lacked. It also marks a departure from the norm for Freddie, who plays rhythm guitar on it.

Queen round off the year with a full British tour, ending up at the Hammersmith Odeon on Boxing Day with a show in aid of the people of Kampuchea.

1980 In February 'Save Me' gets to number eleven and the group go back into the studio to finish *The Game*.

The single 'Play The Game' hits the shops in May and also gets to number fourteen. But the new album, released the following month, goes to number one in the charts.

Work starts on the soundtrack for a new movie, *Flash Gordon*, and another American and Canadian tour follows, opening in Vancouver.

In August another single from *The Game* is released. 'Another One Bites The Dust' gets to the top of the US charts and reaches number seven in Britain.

During October and November Queen polish off the *Flash* soundtrack and it is released in December, just after the band leave for a European tour.

1981 The year starts well, with 'Flash', a British number ten single in January.

In February Queen go back to Japan and then move on to South America, where few rock musicians have performed before.

In November Queen's *Greatest Hits* LP begins its long chart life at the top. The same month the band again get to the top of the charts with their Queen/Bowie collaboration, 'Under Pressure', dubbed by Taylor 'one of the very best things Queen have ever done'.

1982 A European tour begins in Gothenburg in April. During the same month the group release another single, 'Body Language', which reaches number twenty-five in Britain.

May sees the release of the album *Hot Space*, which goes gold and gets to number four in the charts.

The band are still on tour in June and a concert at the Milton Keynes Bowl is filmed by Channel Four. After Britain, Queen move on to Canada, America and Japan.

Also in June a single, 'Las Palabras De Amor' is released and reaches number seventeen. In July 'Calling All Girls' is released in America, but it only makes number sixty. The next British single, 'Back Chat', doesn't do well either, only reaching number forty.

1983 The members of Queen choose this year to take a break from the group and concentrate on solo projects. John Deacon plays bass on a single by Man Friday and Jive Junior, 'Picking Up Sounds'. Brian May plays live on stage in Los Angeles with Def Leppard, produces an album by the group Heavy Pettin' and releases a solo album, *Star Fleet Project*. Mercury works on *Mr Bad Guy* in Munich.

1984 January sees a number two single, 'Radio GaGa'. Written by Taylor, it is inspired, he says, by hearing his three-year-old son say 'radio poo poo'. The single is kept from the top spot by Frankie Goes To Hollywood's hit 'Relax', but reaches number one in nineteen different countries.

In February Queen can be seen at the San Remo Song Festival in Italy and the same month the LP *The Works* is released and is a UK number two, becoming Queen's best-selling album after *Greatest Hits*. Taylor says at the time: 'We thought: "Let's give them the works."'

In April the single 'I Want To Break Free' is released and is a number three hit.

In May Queen are at the Golden Rose Festival in Montreux and July sees the release of the single 'It's A Hard Life', which reaches number six.

In August the band embark on a European tour, including four nights at Wembley Arena.

Meanwhile, in September, *We Will Rock You*, a video compilation, is released, as well as 'Love Kills', Mercury's first solo single under his real name, which is to be used on the soundtrack of an updated version of the film *Metropolis*. The Queen single 'Hammer To Fall' is also released and reaches number thirteen.

Perhaps the group's most controversial move comes in October, when they play to sell-out crowds at Sun City, South Africa, a decision which is to attract a great deal of criticism. Brian May explains: 'We're totally against apartheid and all it stands for, but I feel we did a lot of bridge building.'

In November a Queen Christmas single comes out. 'Thank God It's Christmas' reaches number twenty-one.

1985 In January Queen are at the Rock in Rio Festival, following it with a tour of Australia and New Zealand in April and Japan in May.

Mercury's second solo single, 'I Was Born To Love You', is released in April and reaches number eleven. The solo album *Mr Bad Guy*, written and produced by Mercury, reaches number six.

In July Queen play a blistering set at the Live Aid concert and send record sales soaring, justifying May's claim that Queen are 'probably the best live band on earth right now'. But the same month Mercury's third single from the *Mr Bad Guy* album only reaches number fifty-seven.

In September another Freddie solo effort, 'Living On My Own', reaches number fifty.

November sees the release of Queen's single 'One Vision' from the soundtrack of the film *Iron Eagle*. It goes to number seven.

In December a limited edition box set of albums, *The Complete Works*, is released.

1986 In March 'A Kind Of Magic', from the *Highlander* soundtrack, is released as a single and gets to number three.

The title theme of Dave Clark's musical *Time*, sung by Freddie, is released as a single in May and makes number thirty-two. It is one of two tracks he contributes to the cast recording.

June sees the album *A Kind Of Magic* going straight into the charts at number one and the same month the single 'Friends Will Be Friends' gets to number fourteen.

1986 sees the band dazzle one million people on their European

Magic Tour. It starts on 7 June in Stockholm and finishes at Knebworth Park on 9 August – the last show the band were ever to do, and their biggest ever concert in the UK. In between the band make history when they play behind the Iron Curtain on 27 July at the Nepstadion in Budapest, Hungary. In October Who Wants To Live For Ever reaches number twenty-four.

In December Live Magic is released and makes it to number three in the album charts.

1987 sees the band take another year off from recording and touring as Queen. It proves a fertile time for Mercury's solo career. In February he releases a single, 'The Great Pretender', which becomes his biggest solo hit to date reaching number four in May. In May Mercury indulges his passion for the opera and duets with Spanish opera singer Montserrat Caballé at the Ku club on the holiday island of Ibiza. Their single, 'Barcelona', which was adopted by the Spanish Olympic committee as the theme for the Olympics to be held in Barcelona in 1992, hit number eight in November. In the autumn Taylor forms a band called The Cross because he missed touring and he wanted to go on the road during Queen's quiet periods. September sees the release of their first single, 'Cowboys and Indians'

1988 Mercury's operatic career gathers momentum as he joins Caballé on stage in Barcelona in October. But the singer is forced to mime to their hit 'Barcelona', causing controversy. The same month the duo release the album *Barcelona*, which reaches number twenty-five.

A single from the album, *The Golden Boy* is released.

This year also sees the release of the debut album by the Cross, Talyor's new band, and the year ends with May and Deacon joining the band on stage at the Hammersmith Palais.

1989 Mercury's opera career continues. In January he releases a third single from the *Barcelona* album, 'How Can I Go On?', but it only reaches number ninety-five.

In May a single from the forthcoming album *The Miracle* is released. 'I Want It All' makes it to number three. The album itself is released later in the month.

In July the single 'Breakthru' gets to number seven, staying in the charts for seven weeks.

The next single, 'The Invisible Man', is released in August

and gets to number twelve, swiftly followed by the *Rare Live* video.

'Scandal' enters the charts in October, reaching number twenty-five, and in December 'The Miracle' goes in at number twenty-one, but goes no higher.

In December *Queen At The Beeb*, a compilation from 1973, reaches number sixty-seven and the band start work on a new album.

1990 This is the year when press speculation about Mercury's health increases dramatically, despite strenuous denials from the band that he has AIDS.

Thanks to Mercury's gaunt appearance at the BRIT awards in February, the rumours start up again. The band receive an award for their outstanding contribution to music.

In September the Cross release their second album.

In December the video *Queen At Wembley* is released.

1991 The year starts promisingly when the single 'Innuendo' goes straight into the charts at number one.

In February *Greatest Hits* re-enters the album charts and a new album, *Innuendo*, is released, also reaching number one. Queen record some new material.

In March 'I'm Going Slightly Mad' gets to number twenty-two.

In May 'Headlong' gets to number fourteen amid further speculation about Mercury's health.

In October the single 'The Show Must Go On' is released. The morbid nature of the lyrics is commented on, as is the fact that the video is made up of old footage. The last album *Greatest Hits II* is released a month before he dies.

On 23 November Mercury admits he has AIDS and just twenty-four hours later he is dead.

In December Queen are nominated for the best British group award in the 1991 BRIT awards. The same month 'Bohemian Rhapsody' is re-released as a tribute, and again goes to number one. The profits are donated to AIDS research.

ACKNOWLEDGEMENTS

Many people helped in getting this book together. Among those I would particularly like to single out is Louise Johncox, my researcher, who made a sterling and invaluable contribution to the book. Other thanks go to *Daily Mirror* editor Richard Stott, who let me embark on the project, Don Short, my agent, Val Hudson, at my publishers HarperCollins, Chris Britcher for additional music research, and Nick Gibson and Toni Swindells who soldiered on getting my daily column together as the pace of getting a book out so quickly became frantic.

Thanks also to all the people who talked frankly about the Freddie Mercury they knew, among them tony Pike, Reinhold Mack, Barbara Valentin, Dave Clark, Denis O'Regan, Tony Brainsby, Bryn Bridenthal, Roxy Meade, Chris Poole, Phil Symes, Wayne Eagling, Wayne Sleep and Tim Staffell.

Hundreds of newspaper and magazine articles and many books and videos about Mercury and related subjects were used as secondary sources to my own interviews, including the *Daily Mirror*, *Daily Express*, *Rolling Stone*, *Q*, *Vox*, *NME*, *Melody Maker*, *Daily Star*, *Sun*, *Bunte*, *Evening Standard*, *Evening News*, *The Magic Years* video compilation, and Ken Dean's: *Queen The New Visual*. I would like to thank the *Daily Mirror* library and its chief of enquiries Derek Drury for all their efforts.